THE ELEMENTS OF COLOR

A TREATISE ON THE COLOR SYSTEM OF JOHANNES ITTEN
BASED ON HIS BOOK *THE ART OF COLOR*
EDITED AND WITH A FOREWORD AND EVALUATION BY FABER BIRREN

TRANSLATED BY ERNST VAN HAGEN

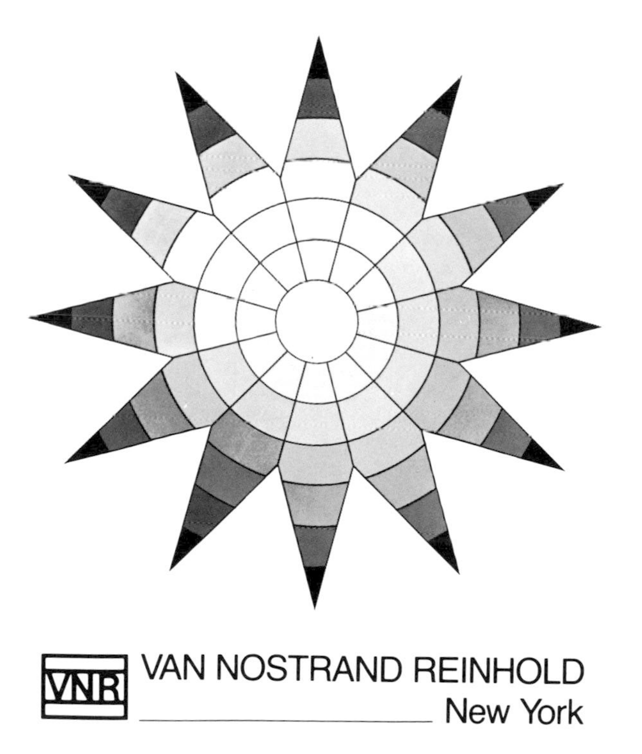

VNR VAN NOSTRAND REINHOLD
New York

Originally published in German under the title KUNST DER FARBE, Studienausgabe
by Johannes Itten

Library of Congress Catalog Card Number 77-124314
ISBN 0-442-24038-4

I Ⓣ P Van Nostrand Reinhold is a division of International Thomson Publishing.
ITP logo is a trademark under license.

Printed in Germany

Published in the United States of America in 1970 by Van Nostrand Reinhold
115 Fifth Avenue, New York, New York 10003

Van Nostrand Reinhold
115 Fifth Avenue
New York, NY 10003

Chapman & Hall GmbH
Pappelallee 3
69469 Weinheim
Germany

Chapman & Hall
2-6 Boundary Row
London
SE1 8HN
United Kingdom

International Thomson Publishing Asia
221 Henderson Road #05-10
Henderson Building
Singapore 0315

Thomas Nelson Australia
102 Dodds Street
South Melbourne, 3205
Victoria, Australia

International Thomson Publishing Japan
Hirakawacho Kyowa Building, 3F
2-2-1 Hirakawacho
Chiyoda-ku, 102 Tokyo
Japan

Nelson Canada
1120 Birchmount Road
Scarborough, Ontario
Canada M1K 5G4

International Thomson Editores
Campos Eliseos 385, Piso 7
Col. Polanco
11560 Mexico D.F. Mexico

97 98 99 RAVEN 30 29 28 27 26

Contents

This present book, *The Elements of Color,* by Johannes Itten, is a simplification and condensation of his major book, *The Art of Color,* published in Germany in 1961. The larger work has been translated into French, Italian, and Japanese. The English edition (also 1961), with the imprint of Van Nostrand Reinhold, is a sizeable volume, 11 ¼ × 12 ¼ inches in size. It has 155 pages, over 100 color illustrations and over 25 in black and white.

In reading Itten and studying his principles and illustrations, the remarkable nature of the man should be appreciated. He was fond of the philosophy of the Far East and studied the wisdom of the ancient Chinese and Hindus. An artist needs inner confidence and self-control and yet must dwell within a real world and be conscious of its interests and requirements. Itten wrote, "We may take warning from the history of India, where, out of preoccupation with exalted spiritual fulfillment, mystics forgot that material life, too, demands cultivation and direction." He recognized the basic laws of color and form, proportions, texture and rhythm as the foundation of his own concept of art education.

This profundity of Itten, by advice and example, draws an effective portrait of the ideal artist. He must be born with some talent, as must a musician or singer. This talent then needs to be developed, enlarged, and perfected through expert training and application. And in the field of color, Itten is a most capable and wise instructor.

There are a number of unusual and original features evident in Itten's work as presented herewith.

First, he has a wide knowledge of art in all nations and among all peoples. He has a keen perception of the genius of the old masters and writes with rare enlightenment on their color expression. He has taken vital part in modern art movements.

He is particularly alert to the remarkable visual effects of simultaneous contrast and offers several dramatic examples in his color plates.

In a chapter on "Subjective Timbre" he calls for personal

feeling. Expression should come from within. "To help a student discover his subjective forms and colors is to help him discover himself." And this Itten strives to do.

In color organization, he describes and illustrates a twelve-part star which he designed in Weimar in 1921. This is amplified by a color circle, a color sphere, and by beautifully graded scales of the twelve colors.

Throughout the book are suggested exercises, which, if carried out, will give a student color control in the sense that practice of music scales will strengthen the facility of a pianist or singer. When creative work is then attempted the student will know what he is about and will not be lost in ignorance or trial and error.

One of the chief features of Itten's contribution to the art of color is his discussion of "The Seven Color Contrasts." These principles compose an important part of his book and, properly absorbed and taken to heart, so to speak, will assure competence and well qualify any student for the rest of his life. The principles may not make a good artist where talent may be lacking, but they will nontheless save him the embarrassment of making clumsy mistakes with the spectrum.

There is sound advice on color mixture, on ways in which hues can be arranged for harmonious order, simple relationships between colors and form, spatial effects.

The book ends with intriguing notes on color symbolism, composition. Any student or artist has the privilege of spending hours, days, or months perusing the conclusions of a great man and profiting from a lifetime of ardent inquiry and understanding.

Johannes Itten (1888–1967)

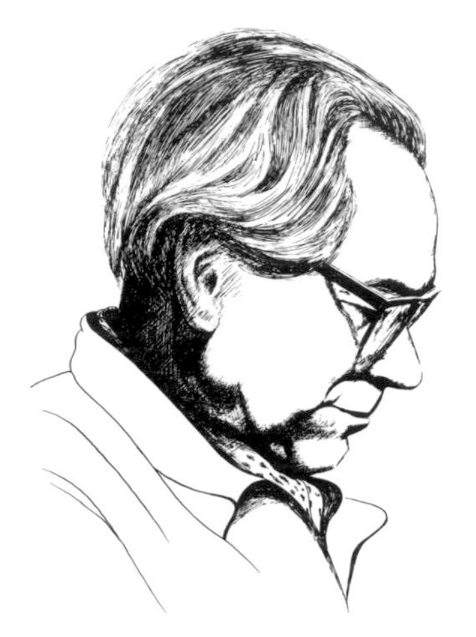

Johannes Itten was considered one of the greatest teachers of the art of color of modern times. Few men of his stature have ever devoted so many years – over five decades – to instruction into the visual, psychological, and esthetic mysteries of color.

He was born near Thun, Switzerland, in 1888. Having a profound interest in painting and color, he went to Stuttgart in 1913 to study under Adolph Hölzel, a leading German color theorist and educator. Fascinated with color, Itten paid scholarly attention to the masterworks of Goethe, Schopenhauer, Runge of Germany, and Chevreul of France. He saw relationships between music and color and gave early attention to abstract color expression in geometrical paintings.

From Stuttgart he went to Vienna where during 1916–1919 he ran his own school. His insistence on spontaneity and personal expression with color – supported by adequate knowledge, discipline, and training – became renowned. In 1919 fourteen of his students followed him to Weimar where he joined the famous Bauhaus founded by Walter Gropius. Here he became a master (1919–1923) and developed the basic course on form and color. Among the other Bauhaus masters were such great artists as Lyonel Feininger, Paul Klee, Oskar Schlemmer and Vasily Kandinsky.

Itten often started his classes with certain oriental exercises and body controls. He wrote, "He who wants to become a master of color must see, feel, and experience each individual color in its many endless combinations with all other colors. Colors must have a mystical capacity for spiritual expression, without being tied to objects."

After leaving the Bauhaus, Itten operated his own school in Berlin (1926–1934) where he formulated many of the principles he later put into book form: *Design and Form, the basic course at the Bauhaus,* published in the United States by Van Nostrand Reinhold. He also founded the School for Textile Design at Krefeld in Germany. Returning to Switzerland, he became director of the Arts and Crafts School-and-Museum of the Textile School at Zurich (1938–1954), and founded the Museum Rietberg.

In addition to many important exhibits in the Arts and Crafts museum, in 1944, long before his major book *The Art of Color* was published, Itten set up special color exhibits in a number of Swiss and German cities.

Itten had always devoted much of his time to painting. Retrospective exhibitions were presented at the Stedelijk Museum in Amsterdam in 1957, at the Kunsthaus, Zürich, in 1964, at the Kunstverein, Düsseldorf, in 1965, and at the Venice Biennal of 1966. He has also been represented in several Bauhaus exhibitions, the most recent being a worldwide traveling exhibition.

Works by Johannes Itten are in the permanent collections of European and American Museums.

Faber Birren

Learning from books and teachers is like traveling by carriage, so we are told in the Veda. The thought goes on, "But the carriage will serve only while one is on the highroad. He who reaches the end of the highroad will leave the carriage and walk afoot."
In this book I shall try to build a serviceable conveyance that will help all who are interested in the problems of color artistry. One may travel carriageless and by unblazed trails, but progress is then slow and the journey perilous. If a high and distant goal is to be attained, then it is advisable to take a carriage at first in order to advance swiftly and safely.
Many of my students have helped me to find materials with which to build, and I am deeply indebted to them.
The doctrine to be developed here is an aesthetic color theory originating in the experience and intuition of a painter. For the artist, effects are decisive, rather than agents as studied by physics and chemistry. Color effects are in the eye of the beholder. Yet the deepest and truest secrets of color effect are, I know, invisible even to the eye, and are beheld by the heart alone. The essential eludes conceptual formulation.

In the realm of aesthetics, are there general rules and laws of color for the artist, or is the aesthetic appreciation of colors governed solely by subjective opinion? Students often ask this question, and my answer is always the same: "If you, unknowing, are able to create masterpieces in color, then un-knowledge is your way. But if you are unable to create masterpieces in color out of your unknowledge, then you ought to look for knowledge."
Doctrines and theories are best for weaker moments. In moments of strength, problems are solved intuitively, as if of themselves.
Close study of the great master colorists has firmly convinced me that all of them possessed a science of color. For me, the theories of Goethe, Runge, Bezold, Chevreul and Hölzel have been invaluable.

I hope to be able to resolve a great many color problems in this book. We are not merely to expound objective principles and rules, but also to explore and survey the subjective predicament, as it pertains to critical taste in the realm of color.
We can be released from subjective bondage only through knowledge and awareness of objective principles.
In music, the theory of composition has long been an important and accepted part of a professional education. However, a musician may know counterpoint and still be a dull composer, if he lacks insight and inspiration. Just so, a painter may know all the resources of composition in form and color, yet remain sterile if inspiration be denied him.

It has been said that genius is 99 per cent perspiration and 1 per cent inspiration. There was a debate in the press years ago between Richard Strauss and Hans Pfitzner about the relative shares of inspiration and contrapuntal deduction in the process of composition.

Strauss wrote that four to six bars were inspiration in his own works, and the rest elaboration. Pfitzner replied, "It may well be that Strauss is inspired only through four to six bars, but I have noticed that Mozart often composes many pages together under inspiration."

Leonardo, Dürer, Grünewald, El Greco and the rest did not scorn to examine their artistic media intellectually. How could the Isenheim altarpiece, now at Colmar, Upper Alsace, France, have been produced, had not its creator pondered form and color?

Delacroix wrote, "The elements of color theory have been neither analyzed nor taught in our schools of art, because in France it is considered superfluous to study the laws of color, according to the saying 'Draftsmen may be made, but colorists are born.' Secrets of color theory? Why call those principles secrets which all artists must know and all should have been taught?" (Les Artistes de mon Temps.)

Knowledge of the laws of design need not imprison, it can liberate from indecision and vacillating perception. What we call laws of color, obviously, can be no more than fragmentary, given the complexity and irrationality of color effects.

In the course of time, the human mind has penetrated many mysteries in their essence or in their mechanism – the rainbow, thunder and lightning, gravity and so on. But they are still mysteries for all that.

As the tortoise draws its limbs into its shell at need, so the artist reserves his scientific principles when working intuitively. But would it be better for the tortoise to have no legs?

Color is life; for a world without colors appears to us as dead. Colors are primordial ideas, children of the aboriginal colorless light and its counterpart, colorless darkness. As flame begets light, so light engenders colors. Colors are the children of light, and light is their mother. Light, that first phenomenon of the world, reveals to us the spirit and living soul of the world through colors.

Nothing affects the human mind more dramatically than the apparition of a gigantic color corona in the heavens. Thunder and lightning frighten us; but the colors of the rainbow and the northern lights soothe and elevate the soul. The rainbow is accounted a symbol of peace.

The word and its sound, form and its color, are vessels of a transcendental essence that we dimly surmise. As sound lends sparkling color to the spoken word, so color lends psychically resolved tone to form.

The primeval essence of color is a phantasmagorical resonance, light become music. At the moment when thought, concept, formulation, touch upon color, its spell is broken, and we hold in our hands a corpse.

In the tinted monuments of past ages, we can trace the emotional dispositions of vanished peoples. The ancient Egyptians and Greeks greatly delighted in varicolored design.

The Chinese were accomplished painters from early times. An emperor of the Han dynasty is recorded in 80 B.C. to have kept storehouses – a museum – of paintings collected by him, said to have been of great and colorful beauty. In the T'ang period (618–907 A.D.), there arose a strongly colored mural and panel painting. About the same time, new yellow, red, green and blue ceramic glazes were developed. In the Sung dynasty (960–1279 A. D.), the sense of color was extraordinarily cultivated. Pictorial colors became more varied and at once more naturalistic. Ceramics evolved many new glazes of matchless beauty, such as celadon and clair de lune.

Strongly colored Roman and Byzantine polychrome mosaics from the first millennium of the Christian era have been preserved in Europe. Mosaic art placed high demands on coloristic powers, because each color area is composed of numerous point elements, each requiring consideration and choice. The mosaic artists of Ravenna in the fifth and sixth centuries were able to produce many different effects with complementary colors.

The mausoleum of Galla Placidia, now at Ravenna, Italy, is dominated by a remarkable colored atmosphere of gray light. This effect is produced by bathing the blue mosaic walls of the interior in an orange light, filtered through narrow windows of orange-tinted alabaster. Orange and blue are complementary colors, the mixing of which yields gray. As the visitor moves about the shrine, he receives different quantities of light, which is alternately accented blue and orange, the walls reflecting these colors at ever-changing angles. This interplay gives an impression of suffusion with color.

In the early medieval illuminations of the Irish monks in the eighth and ninth centuries, we find a palette of great variety and subtlety. Most astonishing in their radiant power are those pages where the many different colors are rendered in equal brilliance. The resulting vivid cold-warm effects are such as we do not find again until the Impressionists and Van Gogh. Some leaves of the Book of Kells, for logic of chromatic execution and organic rhythm of line, are as magnificent and pure as a Bach fugue. The sensitivity and artistic intelligence of these "abstract" miniaturists had their monumental counterpart in the stained glass of the Middle Ages. Early stained glass employed only a few different colors, and therefore seems crude, for glassmaking techniques afforded few colors as yet. Anyone who has spent a day studying the windows in the cathedral at Chartres in the changing light, and has seen the setting sun kindle the great rose window to a splendid culminating chord, will never forget the supernal beauty of that moment.

The Romanesque and Early Gothic artists, in their mural and tablet paintings, used colors as symbolic expressions. Therefore they endeavored to produce unequivocal, unclouded tones. Simple and clear symbolic effect was sought, rather than multitudinous shadings and chromatic variations. Form received a similar treatment.

Giotto and the Sienese school may have been the first painters to individualize the human figure in form and color, thus initiating a development that was to lead to the imposing throng of artist personalities encountered in the Europe of the fifteenth, sixteenth and seventeenth centuries.

In the first half of the fifteenth century, the brothers Hubert and Jan van Eyck began to construct patterns of composition around the local colors of the person or thing represented. These local colors, through dull and bright, light and dark tones, produced realistic images very closely approaching nature. Color became a means of characterizing natural objects. The Ghent altarpiece was finished in 1432, and in 1434 Jan van Eyck executed the first Gothic portrait, the double portrait of Arnolfini and his lady.

Francesca (1410–1492) painted individuals in sharp outline and clearly expressive areas, with balancing complementary colors. The hues are rare tones especially characteristic of the artist.

Leonardo (1452–1519) rejected strong coloration. He painted in infinitesimal tonal gradations, organized in the case of his "Virgin of the Grotto" into two principal planes. "St. Jerome" and the "Adoration" are composed entirely in sepia tones of light and shade.

Titian (1477–1576) in his early work set homogeneous color areas against each other in isolation. Later, he progressively resolved such areas into cool and warm, light and dark, dull and intense modulations, perhaps best exemplified by the "Bella", in the Pitti galleries of Florence, Italy. In the works of his old age, he evolved objects out of one principal hue and many variant tints and shades. The "Ecce Homo" is an example.

El Greco (1545–1614) was a pupil of Titian. He brought his master's polytonality back to large, expressive color areas. His strange, frequently shocking color renditions cease to represent local colors, but are abstract, matching the psychically expressive requirements of the theme. This is why El Greco is considered a progenitor of non-objective painting. His color areas do not denote objective categories. They have been organized into sheer pictorial polyphony.

Grünewald (1475–1528), a century earlier than El Greco, solved the same problem. But where El Greco's tones are always very sharply and individually bounded by grays and blacks, Grünewald set color against color. Through what may be called an objective mastery of the universe of color, he discovered the appropriate colors for each pictorial motif. The Isenheim altarpiece in all its parts shows such multiplicity of color quality, effect and expression as to be properly called an intellectually universal color composition. The Annunciation, Angel Choir, Crucifixion, Resurrection, are pictures utterly different from each other, in form as well as color.

In fact, Grünewald sacrificed decorative unity of the altarpiece as a whole to artistic truth of the individual theme. He set himself above the scholastic canon, in order to be truthful and objective. However, the psychologically expressive power of his colors, their symbolic verity, and their realistic signification – all these three potentialities of color are, in a deeper sense, fused into unity.

Rembrandt (1606–1669) is considered the exemplar of chiaroscuro painters. Though Leonardo, Titian and El Greco used chiaroscuro as a means of expression, Rembrandt's work is altogether different. He felt color as a dense material. With gray and blue or yellow and red transparent tones, he created an effect of depth that has a remarkably transfigured life of its own. Employing a mixed paste of tempera and oil paints, he achieved textures radiating an uncommonly affecting realism. In Rembrandt, color becomes materialized light-energy, charged with tension. Pure colors often shine like jewels in dull settings.

El Greco and Rembrandt carry us into the problems of baroque color. In the more extreme baroque architectures, static space is resolved into space with dynamic rhythm. Color is enlisted in the same service. It is detached from its objective denotation and becomes an abstract means of rhythmic articulation. Ultimately, it is used to assist depth illusions. The work of the Viennese painter Maulpertsch (1724–1796) exhibits such characteristically baroque coloration.

In the art of the Empire and Classical periods, coloration is confined to black, white, gray, sparingly enlivened with some few chromatic colors. This style, giving an effect of realism and sobriety, was supplanted by Romanticism. The beginning of the Romantic movement in painting is identified with Turner (1775–1851) and Constable (1776–1837) in England. Its greatest exponents in Germany were Caspar David Friedrich (1774–1840) and Philipp Otto Runge (1777–1810). These painters employed color as psychico-expressive medium, to lend "mood" to landscape. Constable, for example, would not apply homogenous green to canvas, but would resolve it into minute gradations of light and dark, cold and warm, dull and vivid tones. Color areas were thus rendered subtly vital. Turner produced some non-objective color compositions that would warrant listing him as the first "abstractionist" among European painters.

Delacroix (1798–1863) saw Turner's and Constable's work when he was in London. Their colorism interested him deeply, and on his return, he re-did some paintings of his own in the same spirit, thereby causing a sensation at the 1820 Salon de Paris. Delacroix was actively concerned with color problems and principles throughout his lifetime.

General interest in the influence and rationale of color prevailed early in the nineteenth century. Runge published his color theory using the sphere as a coordinate system in 1810. Goethe's major work on color appeared likewise in 1810, and in 1816 Schopenhauer published his treatise "On Vision and Colors". The chemist M. E. Chevreul (1786–1889), dyemaster of the Gobelin works in Paris, published his "De la Loi du Contraste Simultané des Couleurs et de l'Assortiment des Objets Coloris" in 1839. This work was to become the scientific foundation of Impressionist and Neo-Impressionist painting.

The Neo-Impressionists divided color areas into point elements. They affirmed that mixing pigments breaks the power of the colors. The dots of pure color were to become mingled only in the eye of the viewer.
The color theories of Chevreul were of signal aid to the Impressionists.

Intensive study of nature led the Impressionists to an entirely new color rendition. Study of sunlight, which alters the local tones of natural objects, and study of light in the atmospheric world of landscape, provided the Impressionist painters with new essential patterns. Monet (1840–1926) explored these phenomena conscientiously, requiring a fresh canvas to represent a landscape at each hour of the day, so that the progress of the sun and resulting change in color of the light and reflections might be truly rendered. The best demonstration of this procedure are his cathedral paintings, on display in the Jeu de Paume Museum in Paris.

Proceeding from Impressionist ideas, Cézanne (1839–1906) arrived at a logically developed color construction. It was his task to fashion Impressionism into something "substantial"; his pictures were to stand upon formal and chromatic principle. Apart from his rhythmic and formal contributions, in color he rejected the Pointillist technique of division, returning to continuous areas modulated internally. To him, modulating a color meant varying it between cold and warm, light and dark, or dull and intense. Such modulation throughout the picture area accomplished new, vivid harmonies.
Titian and Rembrandt had contented themselves with color modulations of faces and figures; Cézanne was now integrating the whole picture formally, rhythmically and chromatically. In the still life "Apples and Oranges" this new integration is clearly apparent. Cézanne wished to remold nature at a higher level. To do this, he employed the cold-warm contrast with musical, ethereal effect. Cézanne, and Bonnard after him, composed some pictures entirely on the cold-warm theme.
Matisse refrained from modulation, to again express simple, luminous areas in subjective equilibrium. With Braque, Derain and Vlaminck, he belonged to the Paris group Les Fauves.

The Cubists – Picasso, Braque and Gris – used colors for their light-dark values. They were primarily interested in form. They analyzed the shapes of objects into abstract geometric forms, obtaining relief-like effects by tonal gradation.

The Expressionists – Munch, Kirchner, Heckel, Nolde, and the Blauer Reiter painters Kandinsky, Marc, Macke, Klee – were attempting to restore psychological content to painting. Their creative aim was to represent internalized and spiritualized experience by means of shapes and colors.
Kandinsky began painting non-objective pictures about 1908. He contended that every color has its proper expressional value, and that it is therefore possible to create meaningful realities without representing objects.

Adolf Hölzel became the center of a group of young painters in Stuttgart who attended his lectures on color theory, based on the discoveries of Goethe, Schopenhauer and Bezold.

Between 1912 and 1917, in various parts of Europe independently, artists were at work producing what may be subsumed under the collective name "art concret". Among them were Kupka, Delaunay, Malewitsch, Itten, Arp, Mondrian, and Vantongerloo. Their paintings represent non-objective, usually geometric forms and pure spectral colors in the guise of actual corporeal objects. The intellectually apperceptible forms and colors are media that admit of clear pictorial arrangement.

More recently, Mondrian made a further contribution. He used pure yellow, red, and blue, like weights, to construct paintings whose form and color coincide in the effect of static equilibrium. He aimed not at surreptitious expression, nor at intellectual symbolism, but at real, optically distinct, concrete harmonic patterns.
The Surrealists – Max Ernst, Salvador Dali and the others – have employed colors as means of expression for the pictorial realization of their "irrealities."

Developments in color chemistry, fashion, and color photography have aroused a broad general interest in colors, and the color sensitivity of the individual has been greatly refined. But this contemporary interest in color is almost wholly visual, material in character, and not grounded in intellectual and emotional experience. It is a superficial, external toying with metaphysical forces.
Colors are forces, radiant energies that affect us positively or negatively, whether we are aware of it or not. The artists in stained glass used color to create a supramundane, mystical atmosphere which would transport the meditations of the worshiper to a spiritual plane. The effects of colors should be experienced and understood, not only visually, but also psychologically and symbolically.
The problems of color can thus be examined from several aspects.

The physicist studies the nature of the electromagnetic energy vibrations and particles involved in the phenomena of light, the several origins of color phenomena such as the prismatic dispersion of white light, and the problems of pigmentation. He investigates mixtures of chromatic light, spectra of the elements, frequencies and wave lengths of colored light rays. Measurement and classification of colors are also topics of physical research.

The chemist studies the molecular structure of dyes and pigments, problems of color fastness, vehicles, and preparation of synthetic dyes. Color chemistry today embraces an extraordinarily wide field of industrial research and production.

The physiologist investigates the various effects of light and colors on our visual apparatus – eye and brain – and their anatomical relationships and functions. Research on light- and dark-adapted vision and on chromatic color vision occupies an important place. The phenomenon of afterimages is another physiological topic.

The psychologist is interested in problems of the influence of color radiation on our mind and spirit. Color symbolism, and the subjective perception and discrimination of colors, are important psychological problems. Expressive color effects – what Goethe called the ethico-aesthetic values of colors – likewise fall within the psychologist's province.

The artist, finally, is interested in color effects from their aesthetic aspect, and needs both physiological and psychological information.
Discovery of relationships, mediated by the eye and brain, between color agents and color effects in man, is a major concern of the artist. Visual, mental, and spiritual phenomena are multiply, interrelated in the realm of color and the color arts.

Contrast effects and their classification are a proper starting point in the study of color aesthetics. The problems of subjectively conditioned color perception are especially pertinent to art education and scholarship, architecture and commercial design.
Color aesthetics may be approached from these three directions:

Impression (visually)
Expression (emotionally)
Construction (symbolically)

It is interesting to notice that in pre-Columbian Peru, the use of color is symbolic in the Tiahuanaco culture, expressional in the Paracas, and impressional in the Chimu.
Among historical peoples, there have been styles using colors as symbolic values only, either to identify social strata or castes, or as symbolic terms for mythological or religious ideas.
In China, yellow, the most luminous color, was reserved to the emperor, the Son of Heaven. None other might wear a yellow garment; yellow was a symbol of supreme wisdom and enlightenment. Again, when the Chinese wear white on occasions of mourning, this signifies an escorting of the departed into the kingdom of purity and of heaven. The white color is not an expression of personal grief; it is worn by way of assisting the dead to a state of perfection.
When a pre-Columbian painter in Mexico put a red-clad figure into his composition, it was understood to pertain to the earth god Xipe-totec and therefore to the eastern sky, with its signification of sunrise, birth, youth and springtime. In other words, the figure was colored red not from considerations of visual aesthetics or to convey emotional expression; its color was symbolic, like a logogram or hieroglyph.

The Roman Catholic hierarchy has its distinguishing symbolic colors, including the cardinal crimson and the papal white. In the observance of ecclesiastical feasts, vestments of prescribed colors are worn. Inevitably, sound religious art makes symbolic use of color.

When it comes to studying the emotionally expressive power of colors, our great masters are El Greco and Grünewald.

The visually impressive component of coloration was taken as the cornerstone of their pictorial work by Velásquez and Zurbarán, by Van Eyck and the still-life and interior painters of the Low Countries, by the Le Nain brothers, and later by Chardin, Ingres, Courbet, Leibl, and others. Leibl, particularly painstaking, narrowly observed the minutest modulations of colors in nature, and painted them as minutely on his canvases. He never worked on a picture unless he had the natural model before him. The painters commonly referred to as Impressionists, such as Manet, Monet, Degas, Pissarro, Renoir, and Sisley, studying the local colors of objects as modified by changing sunlight, at last increasingly neglected local colors and addressed their attention to the color vibrations produced by light on surfaces and in the atmosphere at different times of day.
Only those who love color are admitted to its beauty and immanent presence. It affords utility to all, but unveils its deeper mysteries only to its devotees,

Having spoken of three different points of view for purposes of studying color – constructional, expressional, and impressional – I would not omit to say this: Symbolism without visual accuracy and without emotional force would be mere anemic formalism; visually impressive effect without symbolic verity and emotional power would be banal imitative naturalism; emotional effect without constructive symbolic content or visual strength would be limited to the plane of sentimental expression. Of course every artist will work according to his temperament, and must emphasize one or another of these aspects.

To avoid confusion, I should like to define two terms.
By the quality of a color, I mean its position or location

inside the color circle or solid. Both the pure unclouded colors and all their possible mixtures with each other yield unique chromas. The color green, for example, may be mixed with yellow, orange, red, violet, blue, white, or black, and acquires a specific unique quality by each of these admixtures. Each possible modification of a color effect by simultaneous influences likewise generates specific color qualities.
When we are to specify the degree of lightness or darkness of a color, we may speak of its quantity or brilliance. This is what I occasionally refer to as tonal gradation. Brilliance can be varied in two ways; firstly, by mixing a color with white, black, or gray, and secondly, by mixing it with another color of unlike brilliance.

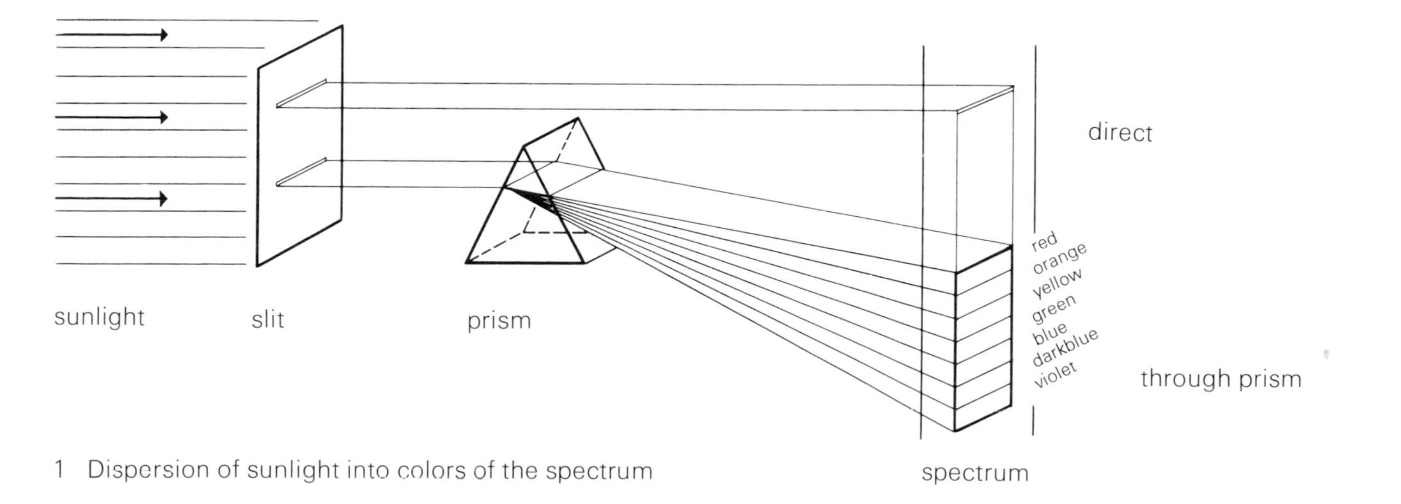

1 Dispersion of sunlight into colors of the spectrum

In 1676, Sir Isaac Newton, using a triangular prism, analyzed white sunlight into a spectrum of colors. Such a spectrum contains all hues except purple.
Newton performed his experiment as follows (Fig. 1): Sunlight entering through a slit falls upon the prism. In the prism, the ray of white light is dispersed into the spectral colors. The dispersed ray of light can be projected on a screen to display the spectrum. A continuous band of color ranges from red through orange, yellow, green, blue, to violet. If this image is collected by means of a converging lens, addition of the colors will yield white light once again.
These colors are produced by refraction. There are other physical ways of generating colors, such as interference, diffraction, polarization, and fluorescence.

If we divide the spectrum into two parts, for example red-orange-yellow and green-blue-violet, and collect each of these two groups with a converging lens, the result will be two mixed colors, whose mixture with each other in turn yields white.
Two kinds of colored light whose mixture with each other yields white are called complementary.
If we isolate one hue from the prismatic spectrum, for example green, and collect the remaining colors – red, orange, yellow, blue, violet – with a lens, the mixed color obtained will be red, i. e. the complementary color of the green we isolated. If we take out yellow, the remaining colors – red, orange, green, blue, violet – will yield violet, the complementary of yellow.
Each spectral hue is the complement of the mixture of all the other spectral hues.
We cannot see the component hues in a mixed color. The eye is not like the musical ear, which can single out any of the individual tones in a mixture.

Colors result from light waves, a particular kind of electromagnetic energy. The human eye can perceive light of wave lengths between 400 and 700 millimicrons only.

1 micron or 1 μ = $^1/_{1000}$ mm. = $^1/_{1000000}$ m.
1 millimicron or 1 $m\mu$ = $^1/_{1000000}$ mm.
The wave lengths and corresponding frequencies, in cycles per second, for each prismatic color, are as follows:

Color	Wave length, $m\mu$	Frequency, cps
Red	800–650	400–470 million million
Orange	640–590	470–520 million million
Yellow	580–550	520–590 million million
Green	530–490	590–650 million million
Blue	480–460	650–700 million million
Indigo	450–440	700–760 million million
Violet	430–390	760–800 million million

The harmonic interval from red to violet is approximately the double; i. e. an octave.

Each hue can be accurately defined by specifying its wave length or frequency. The light waves are not in themselves colored. Color arises in the human eye and brain. How we discriminate these wave lengths is not yet well understood. We know only that the several colors arise from qualitative differences in photosensitivity.
It remains to consider the important question of the colors of objects. If we hold a red and a green color filter, for example, in front of an arc lamp, the two together will give black, or darkness. The red filter absorbs all the rays in the spectrum except for the red interval, and the green filter absorbs all but the green. So no color is left over, and the effect is black. Colors resulting from absorption are known as subtractive colors.
The colors of objects are chiefly subtractive colors of this nature. A red vessel looks red because it absorbs all other colors of light, and reflects only red.
When we say, "This bowl is red", what we are really saying is that the molecular constitution of its surface is such as to absorb all light rays but those of red. The bowl does not have color in itself; light generates the color

If red paper – a surface absorbing all rays but the red – is illuminated with green light, the paper will appear black, because the green light contains no red to be reflected.

All the painter's colors are pigmentary, or corporeal. They are absorptive colors, and their mixtures are governed by the rule of subtraction. When complementary colors, or combinations containing the three primaries, yellow, red, and blue, are mixed in certain proportions, the subtractive resultant is black.
The analogous mixture of prismatic, non-corporeal colors yields white as an additive resultant.

The color agent is the physically or chemically definable and analyzable pigment, the colorant. It acquires human meaning and content by optic and cerebral perception.
The eye and the mind achieve distinct perception through comparison and contrast. The value of a chromatic color may be determined by relation to an achromatic color – black, white, gray – or to one or more other chromatic colors. Color perception is the psychophysiological reality as distinguished from the physicochemical reality of color.
Psychophysiological color reality is what I call color effect. Color agent and color effect coincide only in the case of harmonious polytones. In all other cases, the agency of color is simultaneously transmuted into a new effect. Some examples will demonstrate this.

We know that a white square on a black ground will look larger than a black square of the same size on a white ground. The white reaches out and overflows the boundary, whereas the black contracts.
A light-gray square looks dark on a white background; the same light-gray square looks light on a black ground.

Fig. 58: A yellow square on white and on black. On white, yellow looks darker, with an effect of fine, delicate warmth. On black, yellow acquires extreme brilliance and a cold, aggressive quality of expression.

Fig. 59: A red square on white and on black. Red looks very dark on white, and its brilliance scarcely asserts itself. On black, however, red radiates luminous warmth.
If a blue square is viewed first on white and then on black, the blue on white will give an effect of darkness and depth. The surrounding white square looks brighter than in the case of yellow. On black, the blue takes on a brilliant character, with deep luminescence of hue.
When the effects of a gray square against ice blue and red-orange are compared, the gray on the ice blue

looks reddish, while the same gray on red-orange looks bluish.

When agent and effect do not coincide, we have a discordant, dynamic, unreal, and fugitive expression. It is this power of material and chromatic realities to generate unreal vibrations that affords the artist his opportunity to express the ineffable.

The phenomena instanced might well be grouped under the head of ''simultaneity''. The possibility of simultaneous mutation suggests the advisability, in the process of color composition, of beginning with color effect, and developing the size and shape of areas accordingly.

Once a theme has been conceived, the design must follow that primary and ruling conception. If color is the chief vehicle of expression, composition must begin with color areas, and these will determine the lines. He who first draws lines and then adds color will never succeed in producing a clear, intense color effect. Colors have dimensions and directionality of their own, and delineate areas in their own way.

When people speak of color harmony, they are evaluating the joint effect of two or more colors. Experience and experiments with subjective color combinations show that individuals differ in their judgments of harmony and discord.

The color combinations called "harmonious" in common speech usually are composed of closely similar chromas, or else of different colors in the same shades. They are combinations of colors that meet without sharp contrast. As a rule, the assertion of harmony or discord simply refers to an agreeable-disagreeable or attractive-unattractive scale. Such judgments are personal sentiments without objective force. The concept of color harmony should be removed from the realm of subjective attitude into that of objective principle.

Harmony implies balance, symmetry of forces. An examination of physiological phenomena in color vision will bring us closer to a solution of the problem.

If we gaze for some time at a green square and then close our eyes, we see, as an afterimage, a red square. If we look at a red square, the afterimage is a green square. This experiment may be repeated with any color, and the afterimage always turns out to be of the complementary color. The eye posits the complementary color; it seeks to restore equilibrium of itself. This phenomenon is referred to as successive contrast.

In another experiment, we insert a gray square in an area of pure color of the same brilliance. On yellow, the gray will look gray-violet; on orange, bluish gray; on red, greenish gray; on green, reddish gray; on blue, orange-gray; and on violet, yellowish gray (Figs. 31–36). Each color causes the gray to seem tinged with its complementary. Pure chromatic colors also have the tendency to shift each other towards their complements. This phenomenon is referred to as simultaneous contrast.

Successive and simultaneous contrast suggest that the human eye is satisfied, or in equilibrium, only when the complemental relation is established. Let us approach this idea from a different direction.

In 1797, in Nicholson's Journal, Rumford published his hypothesis that colors are harmonious if they mix to give white. As a physicist, he was speaking in terms of colored light. In the section on color physics, we stated that if one color of a spectrum, say red, is suppressed, and the other colored light rays – yellow, orange, violet, blue, and green – are collected with a lens, the sum of these residual colors will be green, or the complementary of the color suppressed. Physical mixture of a color with its complementary color yields the sum total of the colors, or white; pigmentary mixture yields gray-black.

Ewald Hering, the physiologist, has this to say: "To medium or neutral gray corresponds that condition of the optic substance in which dissimilation – its consumption by vision – and assimilation – its regeneration – are equal, so that the quantity of optic substance remains the same. In other words, medium gray generates a state of complete equilibrium in the eye."

Hering shows that the eye and brain require medium gray, or become disquieted in its absence. If we view a white square on a black ground, and then look away, a black square appears as afterimage. If we look at a black square on a white ground, the afterimage is a white square. The state of equilibrium tends to reestablish itself in the eye. But if we look at a medium-gray square against a gray background, no afterimage differing from the medium gray will appear. Thus medium gray matches the required equilibrium condition of our sense of sight.

Alterations in the optic substance correspond to subjective impressions. Harmony in our visual apparatus, then, would signify a psychophysical state of equilibrium in which dissimilation and assimilation of optic substance are equal. Neutral gray produces this state. I can mix such a gray from black and white, or from two complementary colors and white, or from several colors provided they contain the three primary colors yellow, red, and blue in suitable proportions. In particular, any pair of complementary colors contains all three primaries:

red, green = red (yellow and blue)
blue, orange = blue (yellow and red)
yellow, violet = yellow (red and blue)

So we can say that when a set of two or more colors contains yellow, red, and blue in suitable proportions, the mixture will be gray. Yellow, red, and blue may be substituted for the sum total of colors. Satisfaction of the eye requires this totality, and the eye is then in harmonic equilibrium.

Two or more colors are mutually harmonious if their mixture yields a neutral gray.

Any other color combinations, the mixture of which does not yield gray, are expressive, or discordant, in character. There are many great paintings having a one-sided, expressive intonation, and their color composition is not harmonious, in the sense here defined. Their one-sided, emphatic use of a particular color and its expression has an exciting and provocative effect. Thus not all color composition needs be harmonious, and when Seurat said "Art is harmony," he was mistaking a means of art for its end.

Apart from the relative positions of the colors, of course, their quantitative proportion and their degrees of purity and brilliance are also important.

The basic principle of harmony is derived from the physiologically postulated rule of complementaries. In his Farbenlehre, Goethe writes on the subject of harmony and totality: "When the eye beholds a color, it is at once roused into activity, and its nature is, no less inevitably than unconsciously, to produce another color forthwith, which in conjunction with the given one encompasses the totality of the color circle. A particular color incites the eye, by a specific sensation, to strive for generality. In order, then, to realize this totality, in order to satisfy itself, the eye seeks, beside any color space, a colorless space wherein to produce the missing color. Here we have the fundamental rule of all color harmony."

Color harmony has also been discussed by Wilhelm Ostwald. He writes in his *Primer of Colors,* "Experience teaches that certain combinations of different colors are pleasing, other displeasing or indifferent. The question arises, what determines the effect? The answer is: Those colors are pleasing among which some regular, i. e. orderly, relationship obtains. Lacking this, the effect will be displeasing or indifferent. Groups of colors whose effect is pleasing, we call harmonious. So we can set up the postulate, Harmony = Order.

"To discover all possible harmonies, we must catalogue the possible instances of order in the color solid. The simpler the order, the more obvious or self-evident the harmony. Of such orders, we have found chiefly two: namely the color circles of equal shade (colors of like brilliance or like darkness) and the triangles of like hue (that is, the possible mixtures of a color with white or black). The circles of like shade yield harmonies of different hues, the triangles yield harmonies of like hue."

Where Ostwald says, "colors whose effect is pleasing, we call harmonious", he implies a subjective criterion of harmony. But the concept of harmony should be removed from the realm of subjective attitude to that of objective principle, as I said previously.

Where Ostwald says, "Harmony = Order", and gives the color circles of equal shade and the color triangles of like hue as instances of order, he neglects the physiological laws of afterimage and simultaneity.

One essential foundation of any aesthetic color theory is the color circle, because that will determine the classification of colors. The color artist must work with pigments, and therefore his color classification must be constructed in terms of the mixing of pigments. That is to say, diametrically opposed colors must be complementary, mixing to yield gray. Thus in my color circle, the blue stands opposite to an orange; upon mixing, these colors give gray. In Ostwald's color circle, the blue stands opposite to a yellow, the pigmentary mixture yielding green.

Having provided ourselves with a definition of harmony, let us proceed to the quantitative relationships among colors in harmonious composition. Goethe estimated the luminosities of the primary colors, and derived the following proportionality of areas: yellow:red:blue = = 3:6:8

We can make the general statement that all complementary pairs, all triads whose colors form equilateral or isosceles triangles in the twelve-member color circle, and all tetrads forming squares or rectangles, are harmonious (Fig. 2).

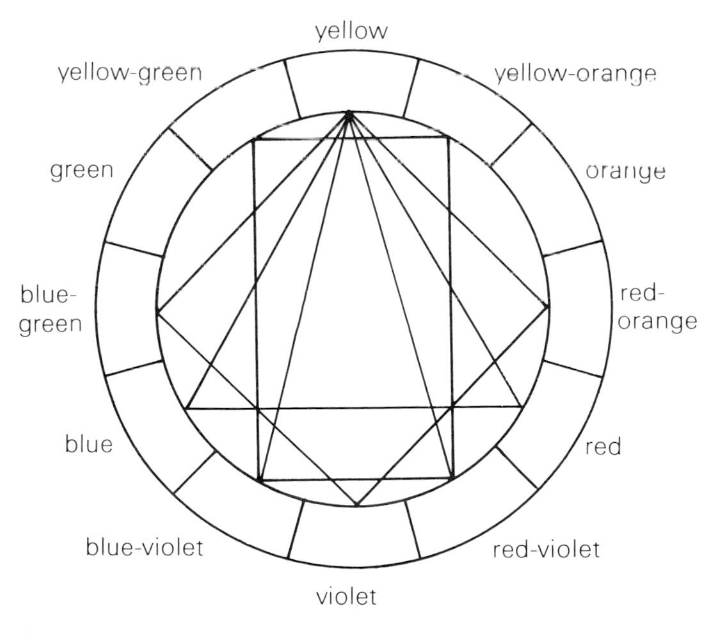

2 Constructions for color chords

Locating the hues yellow, red, blue on the twelve-part color circle, we get an equilateral triangle. This triad expresses the highest intensity and force of color. In the combination, each has its static effect; that is, the yellow acts as yellow, the red as red, the blue as blue. The eye demands no additional, completing colors, and the mixture of the three is a dark gray-black.

Examples of harmonius tetrads are yellow/red-orange/violet/blue-green and the hues of the harmonious rectangle yellow-orange/red-violet/blue-violet/yellow-green.

The geometrical figures used – equilateral and isosceles triangles, square and rectangle – may of course be drawn from any given point on the circle. I can rotate them on the circle, thus replacing the triangle yellow/red/blue by the triangle yellow-orange/red-violet/blue-green, or the triangle orange/violet/green, or the triangle red-orange/blue-violet/yellow-green.

I can do the same with the other geometrical figures. Further discussion will be found in the section on harmonic variations.

In 1928, I was assigning harmonic color combinations to an art class. They were to be painted into complete circular areas, in sectors of unspecified size. I had not yet offered any definition of color harmony. After working away for twenty minutes or so, the class became very restless. I inquired what was the matter, and was told, "We all think that the combinations you assigned are not harmonious. We find them discordant and unpleasant."

I replied, "All right, let each of you paint whatever combinations he finds pleasant and harmonious."

The class quieted down at once, all eager to prove to me that my color combinations were wrong.

After an hour, I had the finished sheets spread out on the floor for inspection. Each student had painted several original, closely similar combinations on his sheet. But each student's work was very different from the others.

It was realized with astonishment that each had his own private conception of color harmony.

In closing this interesting session, I remarked, "The color combinations constructed as harmonious by each individual here represent individual subjective opinion. This is subjective color."

That early observation was to be followed by many more in ensuing years, and I have a large body of documentation in my possession today.

In order for his type of experiment to be successful, the painter must first have been sensitized to color generally. Without prior intensive study of the palette, and practice with brush and paints, reliable results cannot be obtained.

Experiments in subjective color should be initiated very carefully. Any suggestion that subjective color may reveal character or mode of thought and feeling should be avoided. Many people have inhibitions about showing themselves as they are. Anyone who works with color in his vocation is likely to have difficulty in discovering his subjective colors. Again, early

attempts at color combinations are frequently wish fulfillments; subjects paint their complementary colors, or combinations in commercial vogue, instead of reflecting themselves.
Harmonies may be very close, with only two or three colors appearing, as light blue, medium gray, white and black, or dark brown-red, light brown-red and black, or yellow-green, yellow and black-brown, et cetera.
Again, their scope may be very wide – yellow, red, blue, in many degrees of saturation, also two or more pure colors in many different shades.
Between people with very narrow and very wide color scales, there are all conceivable intermediate positions.
There are subjective combinations in which one hue dominates quantitatively, all tones having accents of red, or yellow, or blue, or green, or violet, so that one is tempted to say that such-and-such a person sees the world in a red, yellow, or blue light. It is as if he saw everything through tinted spectacles, perhaps with thoughts and feelings correspondingly colored.
In my studies of subjective color, I have found that not only the choice and juxtaposition of hues but also the size and orientation of areas may be highly characteristic. Some individuals orient all areas vertically; others stress the horizontal or diagonal. Orientation is a clue to mode of thought and feeling. Some individuals incline towards crisp and sharply bounded color areas, others to interpenetrating or blurred and haphazard patches. Individuals of the latter kind are not given to clear and simple thinking. They may be quite emotional and sentimentally disposed.

In any attempt to account for subjective color, we must attend to the most minute traits; but the essential factor is the "aura" of the person.

Some examples will illustrate different subjective color types.

Light blond types with blue eyes and pink skin incline towards very pure colors, often with a great many clearly distinguished color qualities. Contrast of hue is the basic feature. Depending on the forcefulness of the individual, the colors may be more or less luminous.
A very different type is represented by people with black hair, dark skin, and dark eyes, for whom black plays an important part in the harmony.

The construction of the painting personality should proceed from its subjectively given predisposition of form and color.
Knowledge of subjective timbres is of great importance in education and in art instruction. Education should naturally give every child the opportunity to evolve organically out of himself. Therefore educators must be able to recognize the aptitudes and potentialities of their pupils. Subjective color combinations are one key to identification of the individual's natural mode of thinking, feeling, and doing. To help a student discover his subjective forms and colors is to help him discover himself. At first the difficulties may seem insurmountable. Yet let us trust in the immanent spirit of the individual.
The teacher's help should be offered sparingly, though certainly with sympathy and love. As a gardener prepares optimal conditions for the growth of his plants, so the educator should provide the child with favorable conditions of mental and physical growth. Such growth will then follow its own inherent directions and forces.
Art education involves two problems: to further and strengthen the learner's individual creative aptitudes, and to teach the general objective rules of form and color, supplemented by studies from nature. Here, too, individual aptitudes will be amplified and enlarged if the topics assigned are akin to the individual's subjective forms and colors.

The blond type should be assigned such subjects as Springtime, Kindergarten, Baptism, Festival of Bright

Flowers, Garden at Morning. Nature subjects should be vivid, without lightdark contrasts.
Good assignments for a dark type would be Night, Light in a Dark Room, Autumn Storm, Burial, Grief, The Blues, etc. Nature studies can be done in charcoal or black and white pigments.
In other words, it is wrong to impose the same standard flower or figure studies on all students. Individual, subjectively slanted assignments are necessary so that students will be able to discover correct solutions intuitively. When a student is presented with themes "alien" to himself, he is forced to deal with them intellectually while as yet lacking the objective knowledge to do so.
After the student has grasped his own color principles, elementary exercises can be given in all the species of form and color contrast. It will then turn out that some individuals have a preference and flair for certain contrasts, and experience difficulty in handling others. Each student needs a grounding in universal principles, whether he likes it or not. They will generate within him natural tensions, prompting new creations.

It is advisable to illustrate each contrast by analyses of paintings from the past and present. A learner benefits greatly when he encounters works that directly challenge and interest him. His favorite pictures become his masters, and he learns where he stands. One individual will feel drawn rather to the exponents of light-dark contrast, another to those of hue, of form, or of architectural composition. The strong colorism of the Expressionists will enlist the preferences of some.

The total personality can rarely be quite comprehended in the subjective concords; sometimes the physical, sometimes the mental, or spiritual is dominant, or any of numerous composites. The emphasis varies with individual temperament and disposition.
Teachers, physicians, and vocational counsellors can draw many valuable inferences from subjective colors.
One student's subjective colors were light violet, light blue, blue-gray, yellow, white, and a touch of black. His fundamental "tone" was hard, cold, and somewhat brittle. When he was discussing his choice of vocation with me, I suggested that he had a natural affinity for metals, particularly silver, and for glass. "You may be right, but I have decided to become a cabinetmaker," he rejoined. He did afterwards design furniture, and incidentally created the first modern steel chair. He ultimately became a highly successful architect in concrete and glass.
Another student's subjective color chords and compositions contained orange-brown, ocher, red-brown and some black. Green, blue, violet, and gray tones were quite absent. When I asked him about his vocation, he said confidently, "I'm going to be a woodworker." He instinctively perceived his natural calling.
The subjective concords of a third student consisted of sonorous light-violet, yellowish, and gold-brown tones. In their arrangement, these colors produced an effect of radiant splendor, suggesting great powers of concentration. The shading of warm yellow into light violet indicated a religious tendency of thinking. He served as sacristan to an important church, and was a consummate engraver in gold and silver besides.
A man cannot do his best except in an occupation that suits him constitutionally, and one for which he possesses the requisite aptitudes.

It is worth mentioning that though I have diligently sought opinions on my color representations of the seasons, I have never yet found anyone who failed to identify each or any season correctly. This convinces me that above individual taste, there is a higher judgment in man, which, once appealed to, sustains what has general validity and overrules mere sentimental prejudice.
This higher judgment is surely a faculty of the intellect. That is why well-disciplined color thinking and a knowledge of the potentialities of colors are necessary to save

us from the one-sidedness and error of coloration informed by taste alone. If we can find objective rules of general validity in the realm of color, then it is our duty to study them.

Among painters, I perceive three different attitudes towards problems of color.
First there are the epigoni, having no coloration of their own but composing after the manner of their teachers or other exemplars.
The second group is that of the "originals" – those who paint as they themselves are. They compose according to their subjective timbre. Though the theme changes, the chromatic expression of their paintings remains the same.
Leonardo has reference to this group in his Trattato della Pittura: "How ridiculous are those painters who give their figures small heads because their own heads are small." What Leonardo was saying of subjective proportion, I would extend to subjective color.
The third group is that of the universalists – artists who compose from inclusive, objective considerations. Each of their compositions, according to the subject to be developed, has a different color treatment. That there should be but few painters in this group is understandable, for their subjective timbre must comprehend the entire color circle, and this happens rarely. Besides, they must possess high intelligence, admitting of a comprehensive philosophy.

If subjective timbre is significant of a person's inner being, then much of his mode of thought, feeling, and action can be inferred from his color combinations. Intrinsic constitution and structures are reflected in the colors, which are generated by dispersion and filtration of the white light of life and by electromagnetic vibrations in the psychophysiological medium of the individual.
When the individual dies, he blanches. His face and body lose color as the light of life is extinguished. The dead soulless matter of the corpse is devoid of chromatic emanation.

Interpretation of subjective color combinations is not to be based on the several chromas and their expressional values alone. The timbre as a whole is of first importance, then the placement of the colors relative to each other, their directions, brilliances, clarity, or turbidity, their proportions, textures, and rhythmic relationships.

Decorators and designers sometimes tend to be guided by their own subjective color propensities. This may lead to misunderstandings and disputes, where one subjective judgment collides with another. For the solution of many problems, however, there are objective considerations that outweigh subjective preferences. Thus a meat market may be decorated in light green and blue-green tones, so that the various meats will appear fresher and redder. Confectionery shows to advantage in light orange, pink, white, and accents of black, stimulating an appetite for sweets. If a commercial artist were to design a package for coffee bearing yellow and white stripes, or one with blue polka-dots for spaghetti, he would be wrong because these form and color features are in conflict with the theme.
Accordingly, gardeners are daily concerned with important problems of form and color. They observe the growth of plants, their shapes and proportions, and the colors of blossoms, foliage and fruit. The soil, surrounding vegetation, rocks, and conditions of light and shade must receive due consideration if plantings are to produce hoped-for effects. One cannot simply choose one's favorite species and colors of flowers. It would be wrong to plant blue larkspur against a brown wooden fence, or yellow flowers in front of a white stone wall, because these backgrounds would detract from the color effect.

Florists are rigidly dependent on the season and on the

varieties available from time to time. Despite these restrictions, they must continually find objectively correct combinations for all sorts of occasions, and they cannot do so on the basis of personal taste alone. The floral décor for a wedding should be joyful; besides passionate reds and pinks, any vivid hues may be included. For a christening, one would never choose dark blue or dark green, but deliberately prefer light, delicate, small blossoms, in colors of white, light blue, pink, light yellow, as well as light green. Called upon to supply floral decorations for the anniversary of an association, the florist would arrange strong colors and large blossoms in ceremonial, rather impersonal combinations, including distinctive green leaf forms, the whole to express disciplined but festive power.

Salespeople whose customers are sensitive to color will be more successful if they try to understand their customers' tastes rather than to impose their own. Every woman should know what colors are becoming to her; these will always be her subjective colors and their complements. When a customer is looking for a certain hue, he needs to know what other colors may strengthen, weaken, or simultaneously modify it. Brightly colored merchandise should not be left within the buyer's field of vision, because it may exert powerful simultaneous influences.

Fashion executives require familiarity with the general, objectively valid principles of form and color. Several times a year, the fashion designer is expected to come up with a new line in the fashionable colors. If these are close to his subjective colors, he will easily discover the tints and shades he needs. His line will be convincing and successful. But if the hues required by fashion are counter to his subjective colors, he will find his task ungrateful and laborious.

If an interior decorator's personal spectrum is dominated by blue-gray, he will "naturally" tend to do all sorts of interiors in blue-gray tones, these being particularly satisfying to himself. Clients who are chromatically "related" to him will be pleased; but those who are attuned to orange, or green, will find their surroundings uncongenial and will feel ill-at-ease.

Nowadays, architects frequently put up great blocks of dwellings in uniform colors. They should realize that only people of corresponding color sense will enjoy these quarters, and that all others will be more or less repelled. Uncongenial colors may constitute a severe stress upon sensitive individuals. Is not generality of well-being a more important aim than aesthetic unity?

These examples all go to show that subjective taste cannot suffice for the solution of all color problems. Knowledge of objective principles is essential to the correct evaluation and use of colors.

Constructive color theory embraces the principles of color effects insofar as they can be derived empirically.

When Rainer Maria Rilke one day asked Rodin, "Cher maître, how would you describe the creative process, from the inception of a project?" Rodin replied: "First I experience an intense feeling, which gradually becomes more concrete and urges me to give it plastic shape. Then I proceed to plan and design. At last, when it comes to execution, I once more abandon myself to feeling, which may prompt me to modify the plan." Cézanne said of himself, "Je vais au développement logique de ce que je vois dans la nature."*
Matisse, seemingly guided mainly by his own feeling, made little sketches of projected paintings, and indicated the selection and distribution of colors in writing, before beginning to paint. In other words, he too, like Rodin and other masters, devised a rationally calculated composition, which he would afterwards use or reject according to his subjective feeling during the course of the work.
Any calculated plan, then, will not be the ruling factor. Intuitive feeling is superior to it, navigating the realm of the irrational and metaphysical, not subject to number. Deliberate intellectual construction is the "conveyance" that carries us to the portals of this new reality.
In order to learn the objective principles of color, take brush in hand and reproduce the charts and exercises in this book. The figures show only elementary examples, and the beginning colorist must do a great many more exercises if he is to progress beyond the theoretical.

* I proceed to a logical development of what I see in nature.

By way of introduction to color design, let us develop the 12-hue color circle from the primaries – yellow, red, and blue. As we know, a person with normal vision can identify a red that is neither bluish, nor yellowish; a yellow that is neither greenish, nor reddish; and a blue that is neither greenish, nor reddish. In examining each color, it is important to view it against a neutral-gray background.

The primary colors must be defined with the greatest possible accuracy. We place them in an equilateral triangle with yellow at the top, red at the lower right, and blue at the lower left.

About this triangle we circumscribe a circle, in which we inscribe a regular hexagon. In the isosceles triangles between adjacent sides of the hexagon, we place three mixed colors, each composed of two primaries. Thus we obtain the secondary colors:

yellow + red = orange
yellow + blue = green
red + blue = violet

The three secondary colors have to be mixed very carefully. They must not lean towards either primary component. You will note that it is no easy task to obtain the secondaries by mixture. Orange must be neither too red, nor too yellow; violet neither too red, nor too blue; and green must be neither too yellow, nor too blue.

Now, at a convenient radius outside the first circle, let us draw another circle, and divide the ring between them into twelve equal sectors. In this ring, we repeat the primaries and secondaries at their appropriate locations, leaving a blank sector between every two colors.
In these blank sectors, we then paint the tertiary colors, each of which results from mixing a primary with

a secondary, as follows:

yellow + orange = yellow-orange
red + orange = red-orange
red + violet = red-violet
blue + violet = blue-violet
blue + green = blue-green
yellow + green = yellow-green

Thus we have constructed a regular 12-hue color circle in which each hue has its unmistakable place (Fig. 3). The sequence of the colors is that of the rainbow or natural spectrum.

Newton obtained a continuous color circle of this kind by supplementing the spectral hues with purple, between red and violet. So the color circle is an artificially augmented spectrum.

The twelve hues are evenly spaced, with complementary colors diametrically opposite each other.
One can accurately visualize any of these twelve hues at any time, and any intermediate tones are easily located.
I think it is a waste of time for the colorist to practice making 24-hue, or 100 hue, color circles. Can any painter, unaided, visualize Color No. 83 of a 100-hue circle?

Unless our color names correspond to precise ideas, no useful discussion of colors is possible. I must see my twelve tones as precisely as a musician hears the twelve tones of his chromatic scale.

Delacroix kept a color circle mounted on a wall of his studio, each color labeled with possible combinations. The Impressionists, Cézanne, Van Gogh, Signac, Seurat, and others, esteemed Delacroix as an eminent colorist. Delacroix, rather than Cézanne, is the founder of the tendency, among modern artists, to construct works upon logical, objective color principles, so achieving a heightened degree of order and truth.

3 Twelve-part color circle, developed from the primary colors yellow/red/blue and the secondary colors orange/green/violet

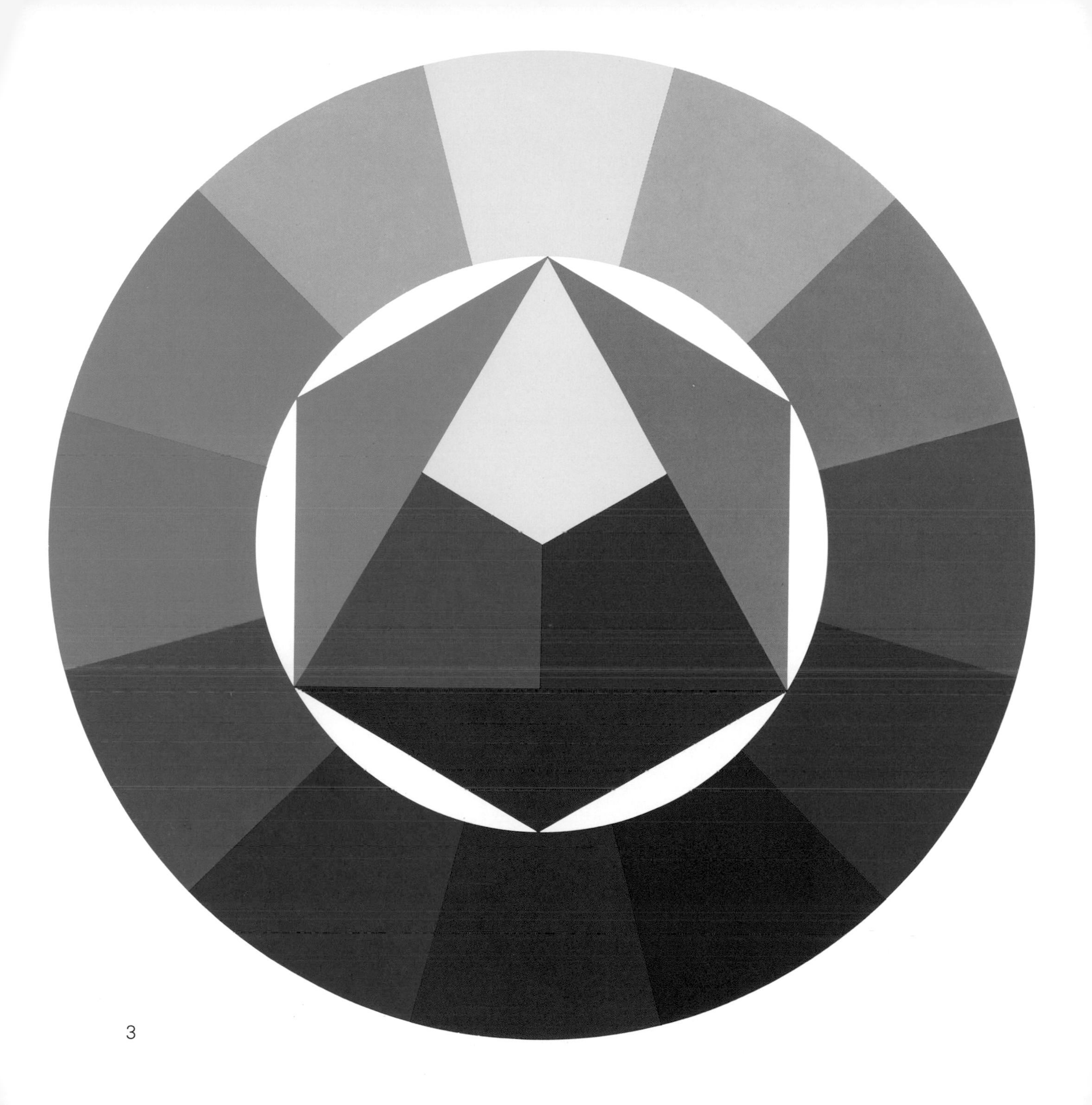

3

We speak of contrast when distinct differences can be perceived between two compared effects. When such differences attain their maximum degree, we speak of diametrical or polar contrasts. Thus, large-small, white-black, cold-warm, in their extremes, are polar contrasts. Our sense organs can function only by means of comparisons. The eye accepts a line as long when a shorter line is presented for comparison. The same line is taken as short when the line compared with it is longer. Color effects are similarly intensified or weakened by contrast.

The physiological problem of contrast effects lies in the special field of aesthesiology, and will not be taken up here.

When we survey the characteristics of color effects, we can detect seven different kinds of contrast. These are so different that each will have to be studied separately. Each is unique in character and artistic value, in visual, expressive, and symbolic effect; and together they constitute the fundamental resource of color design.

Goethe, Bezold, Chevreul, and Hölzel have noted the significance of the various color contrasts. Chevreul devoted an entire work to "Contraste Simultané". However, a systematic and practical introduction to the special effects of color contrast, with exercises, has been lacking. Such an exploration of the color contrasts is an essential part of my course of instruction.

The seven kinds of color contrast are the following:

1. Contrast of hue
2. Light-dark contrast
3. Cold-warm contrast
4. Complementary contrast
5. Simultaneous contrast
6. Contrast of saturation
7. Contrast of extension

Contrast of hue is the simplest of the seven. It makes no great demands upon color vision, because it is illustrated by the undiluted colors in their most intense luminosity. Some obvious combinations are: yellow/red/blue; red/blue/green; blue/yellow/violet; yellow/green/violet/red; violet/green/blue/orange/black.

Just as black-white represents the extreme of light-dark contrast, so yellow/red/blue is the extreme instance of contrast of hue (Fig. 4). At least three clearly differentiated hues are required. The effect is always tonic, vigorous, and decided. The intensity of contrast of hue diminishes as the hues employed are removed from the three primaries.
Thus orange, green, and violet are weaker in character than yellow, red, and blue; and the effect of tertiary colors is still less distinct.
When the single colors are separated by black or white lines, their individual characters emerge more sharply. Their interaction and mutual influences are suppressed to some extent. Each hue acquires an effect of reality, concreteness. Though the triad yellow/red/blue represents the strongest contrast of hue, all pure, undiluted colors of course can participate in this contrast (Fig. 6).
Contrast of hue assumes a large number of entirely new expressive values when the brilliances are varied (Fig. 7). In the same way, the quantitative proportions of yellow, red, and blue may be modified. Variations are numberless, and so are the corresponding expressive potentialities. Whether black and white are included as elements of the palette will depend on subject matter and individual preference. As is shown by the illustrations under Color Agent and Color Effect, white weakens the luminosity of adjacent hues and darkens them; black causes them to seem lighter. Hence white and black may be powerful elements of color composition (Fig. 5).

The same exercises might be worked out in patches of color without preassigned shapes. However, this procedure would involve hazards. The student would start experimenting with shapes instead of studying color areas and tensions. He would draw outlines, and this practice is hostile to color design and should be strictly avoided. In most exercises, we use simple stripe or checkerboard patterns.

The exercise in Fig. 8 shows a checkerboard pattern in yellow, red, blue, white and black. The student is to develop the colors in two spatial directions, to strengthen his sense of tensions between color areas. Fig. 9 shows extremely luminous colors, with tints and shades, as well as white and black. When the harmony of Fig. 6 has been worked out, the student can go on to pick out the colors for the exercise in Fig. 10, locating the most luminous ones.

Very interesting studies are obtained if one hue is given the principal role, and others are used in small quantities, merely as accents. Emphasizing one color enhances expressive character. After each geometrical exercise is carried out, free compositions in the same kind of contrast should be attempted.

There are many subjects that can be painted in contrast of hue. The significance of this contrast involves the interplay of primeval luminous forces. The undiluted primaries and secondaries always have a character of aboriginal cosmic splendor as well as of concrete actuality. Therefore they serve equally well to portray a celestial coronation or a mundane still life.

Contrast of hue is found in the folk art of peoples everywhere. Gay embroidery, costume, and pottery testify to primitive delight in colorful effects. In the illuminated manuscripts of the Middle Ages, contrast of hue was used in manifold variations, often not from motives of aesthetic necessity but out of sheer pleasure in decorative invention.

Contrast of Hue

4 The strongest expression of contrast of hue: yellow/red/blue
5 Yellow/red/blue/white/black
6 Colors of greatest luminosity
7 Same colors as Fig. 6, in tints and shades
8 Checkerboard pattern in yellow, red, blue, white, and black
9 Colors of greatest luminosity with tints and shades, white and black
10 Colors of greatest luminosity

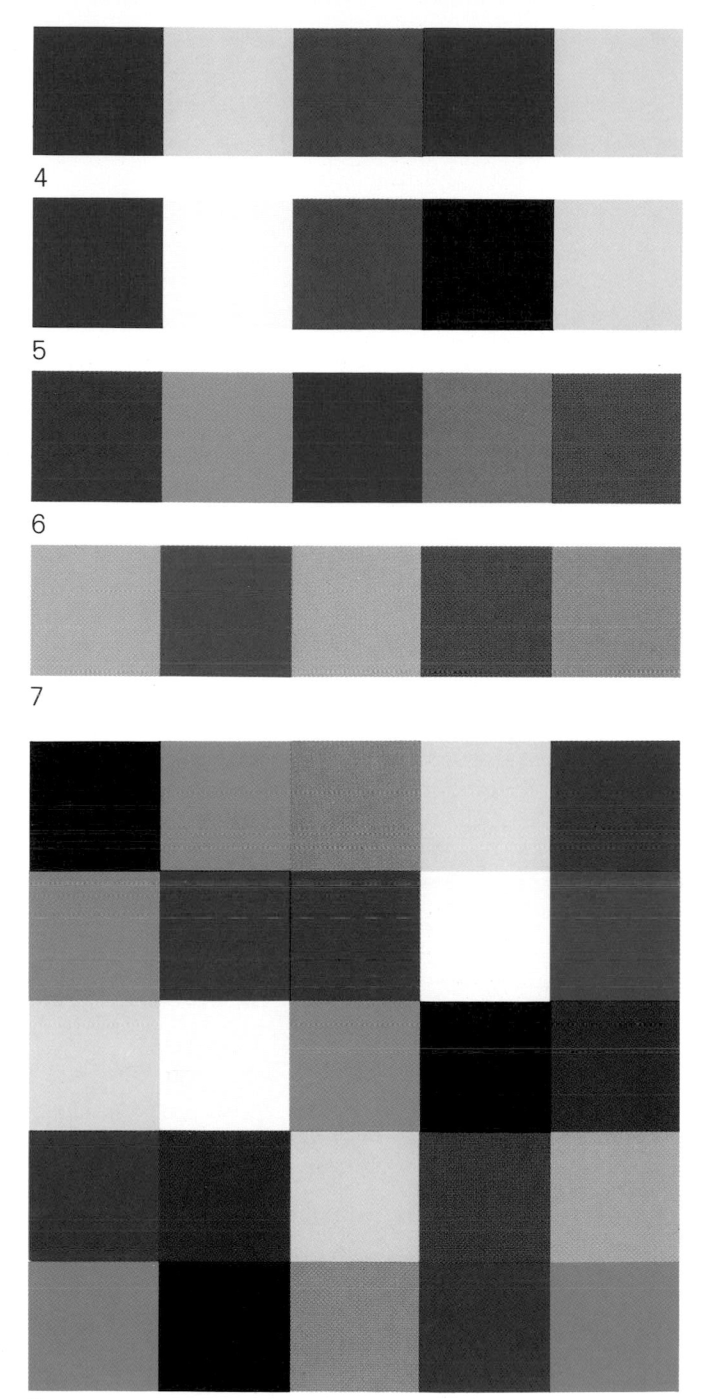

4

5

6

7

8

9

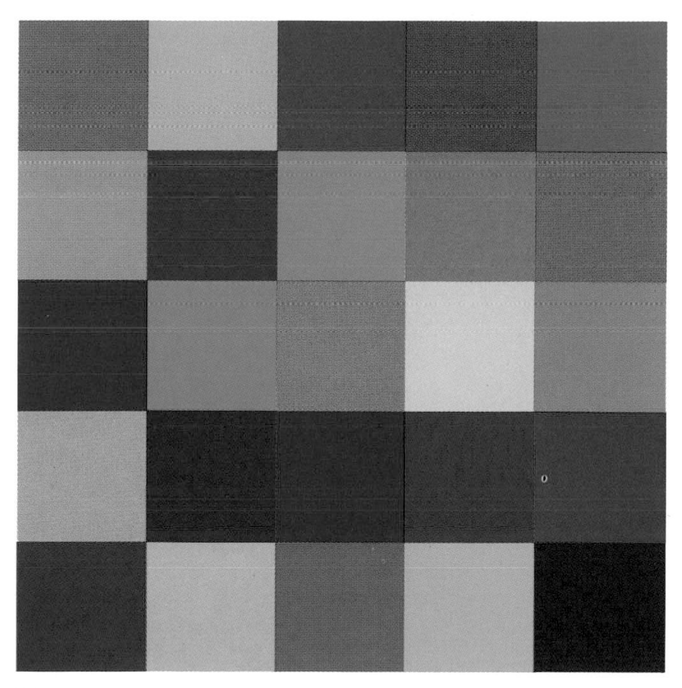

10

Contrast of hue is dominant also in early stained glass, its primordial force actually asserting itself over the plastic form of architecture. Stefan Lochner, Fra Angelico and Botticelli are among painters who have based compositions on contrast of hue.

Perhaps the grandest example of its significant use is Grünewald's "Resurrection", where this contrast displays all of its universalistic power of expression.

So in Botticelli's "Lamentation" (in the Pinakothek, Munich), contrast of hue serves to characterize the all-embracing grandeur of the scene. The totality of hues symbolizes the cosmic significance of the epochal event.

Here we see that the expressive potentialities of one and the same color contrast may be widely diverse. Contrast of hue may alike express boisterous joviality, profound grief, earthy simplicity, and cosmic universality.

Among the moderns, Matisse, Mondrian, Picasso, Kandinsky, Léger, and Miró have frequently composed in this mode. Matisse especially uses it in still-life and figure paintings. A good example is the portrait "Le Collier d'Ambre", painted in the pure colors of red, yellow, green, blue, red-violet, white, and black. This combination expressively characterizes a young, sensitive, and clever woman.

The Blauer Reiter painters Kandinsky, Franz Marc, and August Macke, worked in contrast of hue almost exclusively during their early period.

Among a great many possible examples of the use of contrast of hue, I would suggest these four paintings: "L'Église d'Ephèse" from "Apocalypse de Saint Sever" (11th century), Paris, Bibliothèque Nationale; Enguerrand Charonton's "Coronation of the Virgin" (15th century), Villeneuve-les-Avignon, Hôpital; Paul de Limbourg's "May-Day Excursion" in "Les Tres Riches Heures du Duc de Berry" (1410), Chantilly, Musée Condé; Piet Mondrian (1872–1944), "Composition 1928", Mart Stam Collection.

Day and night, light and darkness – this polarity is of fundamental significance in human life and nature generally. The painter's strongest expressions of light and dark are the colors white and black. The effects of black and white are in all respects opposite, with the realm of grays and chromatic colors between them. The phenomena of light and dark, both among white, black and gray, and among pure colors, should be thoroughly studied, for they yield valuable guides to our work.

Black velvet is perhaps the blackest black, and baryta is the purest white. There is only one maximal black and one maximal white, but an indefinitely large number of light and dark grays, forming a continuous scale between white and black.

The number of distinguishable shades of gray depends on the sensitivity of the eye and the response threshold of the observer. This threshold can be lowered by practice, increasing the number of perceptible gradations. A uniformly gray, lifeless surface can be awakened to mysterious activity by extremely minute modulations of shading. This very important factor in painting and drawing requires extreme sensitivity to tonal differences.

Neutral gray is a characterless, indifferent, achromatic color, very readily influenced by contrasting shade and hue. It is mute, but easily excited to thrilling resonances. Any color will instantly transform gray from its neutral, achromatic state to a complementary color effect corresponding mathematically to the activating color. This transformation occurs subjectively, in the eye, not objectively in the colors themselves. Gray is a sterile neuter, dependent on its neighboring colors for life and character. It attenuates their force and mellows them. It will reconcile violent oppositions by absorbing their strength and thereby, vampirelike, assuming a life of its own.

Delacroix objected to gray for this reason, as injurious

to the power of color.
Gray may be mixed from black and white, or from yellow, red, blue, and white, or from any pair of complementary colors.

First we prepare a regular series of grays from white to black, in twelve steps. It is important to space the steps evenly. The gray of medium brilliance should be in the center of the scale. Each individual step should be perfectly uniform and spotless, with neither a light nor a dark line between it and its neighbors. Similar scales of brilliance can be prepared for any chromatic color. In the blue scale, blue is darkened with black down to blue-black, and lightened with white up to blue-white.

These exercises serve to sharpen the student's sensitivity to shading. The twelve steps are not intended, as in music, to represent a system of "equal temperament." In the art of color, not only precise intervals but inappreciable transitions, comparable to the glissando in music, may be important vehicles of expression.

The following exercises are intended to enlarge comprehension of light-dark contrast.

Certain shades may be selected from the scale of grays obtained, and arranged in any sequence to form a composition. When five or six such compositions have been completed, they are rated comparatively. It is soon realized that some are good and convincing, others poor or false. This very simple exercise will assess a talent for chiaroscuro.

Fig. 11 shows the development of a light-dark combination upon a checkered surface. This composition may be lightened or darkened as a whole; the main point is to cultivate vision and perception of light-dark gradations and their contrasts.
When the problem of white, gray, black tonal values

Light-Dark Contrast

11 Light-dark composition in black, white, and grays
12 Same composition as Fig. 11, in blue
13 Colors of equal brilliance
14 Colors of equal darkness

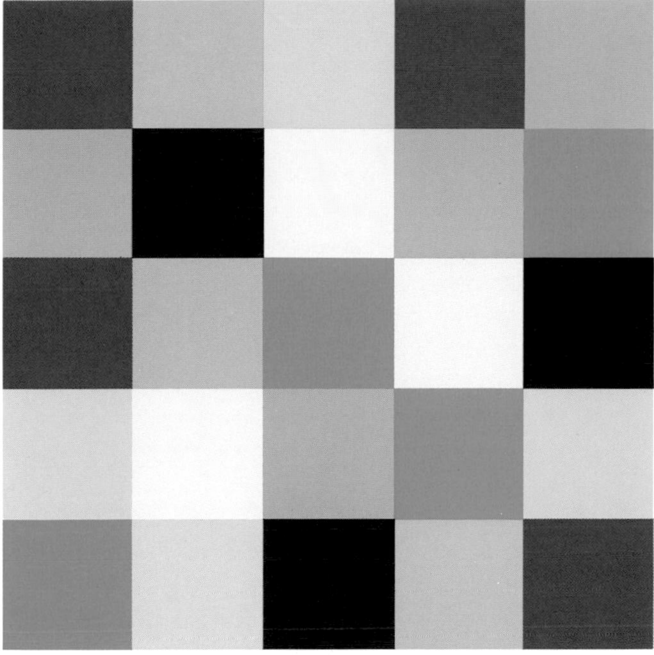

11

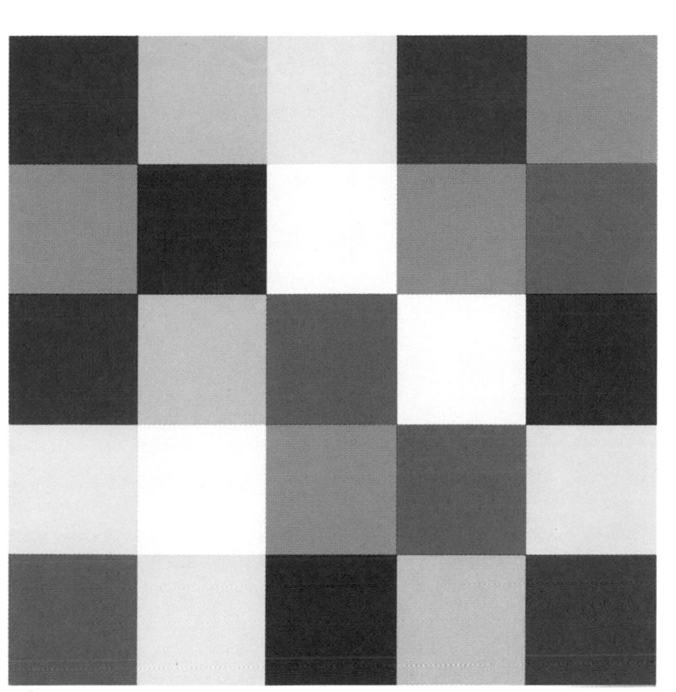

12

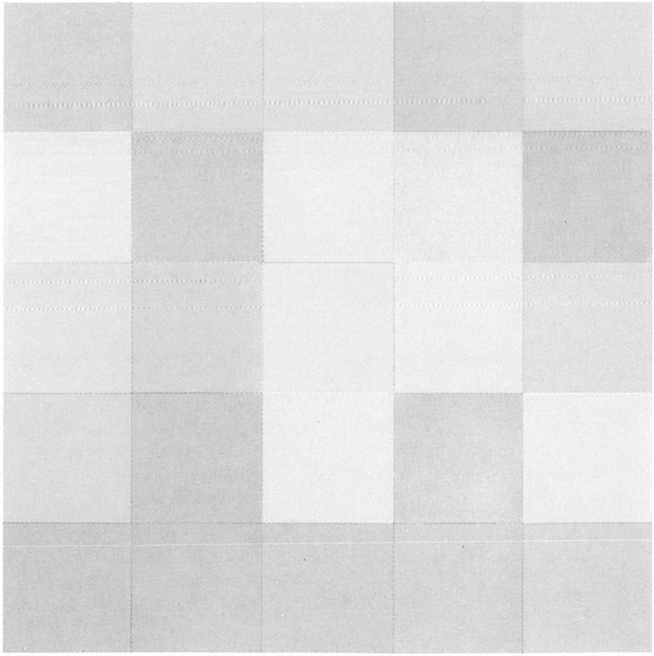

13

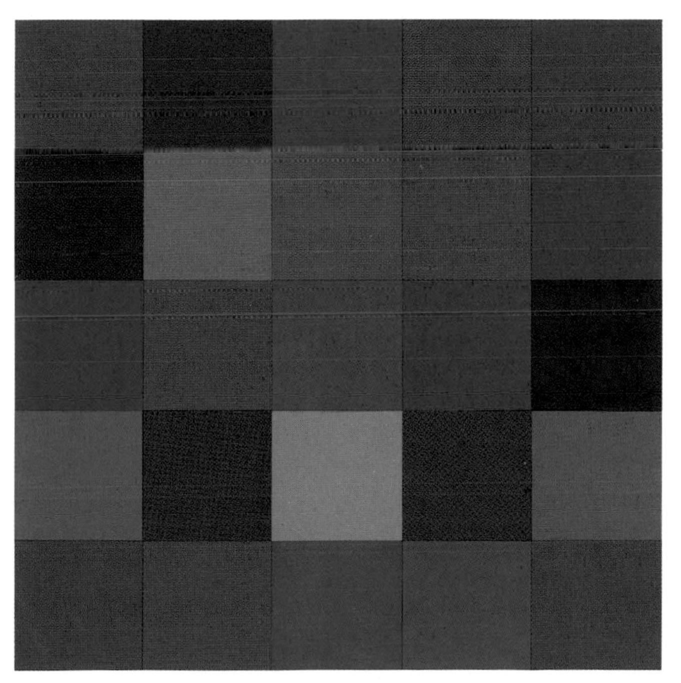

14

has been grasped, contrast of proportion or extension can be added to light-dark contrast.
Contrasts of proportion comprise large-small, long-short, wide-narrow, thick-thin. To gain familiarity with the problems of proportion, the exercises should be done in light-dark, developing not only the feeling for proportion but also for the relation of the positive, dark form to the negative, white form remaining.

Much European and Asian art is constructed upon pure light-dark contrast. Chinese and Japanese ink drawing is an outstanding example. The technique of this art stems from the art of writing in these countries, where ideographic characters, representing a wealth of forms, are made with the brush. Their semantically and rhythmically correct execution requires a repertory of many different manual motions. Sense of form, rhythmic feeling, and relaxed attentiveness are necessary to "correct" brushwork. In China and Japan, writing is a fine art. "When an archer has thoroughly sighted his target, poised his body, grasped his bow firmly, and aimed accurately, the arrow will almost certainly hit the mark. So with the calligrapher: with the mind concentrated, the body upright and balanced, the brush vertical, the dot or stroke should fall exactly on the appointed place." (Chian Yee, "Chinese Calligraphy", Harvard University Press.)

This writing proceeds from an inward automatism. After endless practice, the strokes at last flow effortlessly from the brush; and in the same way, the Chinese or Japanese painter practices the lexicon of nature until he can reproduce it at will. This discipline presupposes mental concentration and physical relaxation. Meditation as practiced particularly in Ch'an, or Zen, Buddhism provides the foundation of this training of mind and body. Accordingly, many monks of this sect are to be found among the great artists in black and white. They did not engage in meditation in order to become great painters; they worked with the brush as an aid to meditative internalization.

Other media of light-dark expression are the woodcut, copperplate, and etching. The artist, by shading and hatching, can produce extremely differentiated gradations of light and dark. Rembrandt's etchings cover a very wide range of subject matter. As is not surprising, he also executed pen-and-ink and brush drawings in masterful chiaroscuro, often rivaling the suggestive power and clarity of East Asian work.
In his numerous sketches, Seurat explored light-dark gradations most conscientiously. Seurat's drawings, like his paintings, give one the feeling that he is devoting thought to each pinpoint in order to evoke the most delicate of shadings.

Thus far, we have considered light-dark contrast only in the range of black, white, and gray. The light-dark evaluation of chromatic colors and their relationships to the achromatic colors – black, white and gray – is far more complicated. The domain of grays extends between white and black, just as the world of colors burns between light and darkness.

Gradations and brilliancies of achromatic colors are easily distinguished, and so are those within each chromatic hue. Difficulties arise when gradations of unlike hues are to be compared. It is most important to be able to identify colors of equal brilliance accurately. The following exercise will help to develop this ability.

In a checkerboard array, we place yellow or red or blue. We are then required to add colors having the same amount of light or dark as the given color. We make a point of using yellowish, bluish, and reddish hues on each attempt. Brilliance must not be confused with the saturation, or purity, of the colors.

Special difficulties are presented by cold and warm colors. Cold colors seem transparent, weightless, and are commonly rendered too light, whereas the warm hues, because of their opacity, tend to be rendered too dark. The exercise of painting all the hues in the same brilliance as yellow is difficult because it is not immediately realized how brilliant yellow is (Fig. 13). It is similarly difficult to render yellow as dark as red or blue. Shading and dilution necessarily deprive brilliant yellow of its yellowness; this naturally disinclines many people to darken yellow. In Fig. 14, all the colors are equal in darkness to the blue.

Equality of light or dark relates colors to each other, tying or bracketing them together. Light-dark contrast between them is extinguished. This is an invaluable resource of artistic design.
In the color sphere, Figs. 49 and 50, both the chromatic colors of the twelve-hue color circle and the achromatic colors are represented. Contrary to the chromatic colors, the achromatic colors produce an effect of the categorical, rigid, incorruptible, and abstract. They are in antithesis to the vibrant complexity of the chromatic colors. Yet it is possible for the achromatic colors to acquire a borrowed chromatic effect. By simultaneous contrast (Figs. 31–36), a neighboring hue may induce an achromatic gray to look like its complementary hue. When achromatic colors occur in a composition and adjoin chromatic colors of like brilliance, they lose their achromatic character.
If the achromatic colors are to retain their condition of abstraction, the chromatic colors must be of different brilliance. In a composition where whites, blacks, and grays are used as means for abstract effect, there should be no chromatic colors matching them in brilliance, or simultaneous contrast will activate the neutrals. But when gray is used as a vivid component in a color composition, then the adjoining chromatic tone must match the gray in brilliance.
The Impressionists were interested in this active function of grays, whereas constructionists and concrete painters use black, white, and gray abstractly.

The problems of light-dark contrast in colors are illustrated by the exercise in Fig. 15. The twelve equidistant steps of gray from white to black in the first row have been repeated for the twelve hues of the color circle, in brilliances equal to the corresponding grays. We see that the pure yellow answers to the threeth step. Orange is at the fifth step, red at the sixth, blue at the eighth, and violet at the ninth step in the scale of grays. The chart shows saturated yellow to be the lightest of the pure colors, and violet the darkest.

Thus yellow must be muted from the fourth step on, in order to match the darker tones of the gray scale. Pure red and blue are at a lower level, leaving few steps to black, but many on the way to white. Each admixture of black or white reduces the vividness of a hue.
Along any horizontal row of the chart, all squares should be of the same brilliance as the corresponding gray.
If we prepare a sequence of as many as eighteen gradations, instead of twelve, and connect the points of highest purity, we can see that the curve is parabolic. The fact that the pure, saturated hues, as they appear in the chart of Fig. 15, differ in brilliance, is extremely important. It must be realized that pure saturated yellow is very light, and that there is no such thing as a dark pure yellow. Saturated essential blue is very dark; light blues are pale and dim. Red can emit its considerable vivid power only as a dark color; red lightened to the level of pure yellow loses all radiance. The colorist positively must allow for these facts in his compositions. When a saturated yellow is to produce the main effect, the composition generally must assume a light over-all character, whereas pure saturated red or blue requires a dark over-all expression. The radiant reds in Rembrandt's paintings are so only because of contrast with yet darker tones. When he wants radiant yellows, he can bring them out in comparatively light groups, where saturated red would be felt as merely dark, without chromatic splendor. Fig. 3 illustrates this principle.
The unlike brilliancies of hues in themselves pose difficult problems for textile designers. Familiarly, any textile design is likely to be produced in four or more differ-

ent colors or combinations. In the group as a whole, these must be somehow coordinated. A fundamental rule is that corresponding areas of the design should produce the same effect of contrast in each version.
Fig. 12 shows a version of Fig. 11 in blue. When a brilliant red occurs in a design, there will not be enough luminous shades on the same level as the red for the six or eight other combinations. But the brilliance intervals should be the same in all color versions. If a luminous orange were to replace the red, the whole color composition would have to be transposed to the brilliance level of the luminous orange. The material in orange would then have to be lighter upon the whole than the material in red. If the orange were put at the brilliance level of the red, the luminous red would correspond to a dim brown-orange, lacking in radiance.
A serious complication is that the light-dark values of the pure colors vary with the intensity of illumination. Red, orange, and yellow look darker in reduced light, while blue and green look lighter. Thus shadings may produce the right effect in full daylight, and yet appear false at twilight. Altarpieces painted for the semi-obscurity of churches, therefore, should not be exhibited under skylights in museums or in the glare of artificial light, since the light-dark values of their colors would be falsified.
The plates and exercises in this book are designed to be viewed in full daylight.

A composition painted in light-dark contrast may be constructed of two, three, or four principal tones. The painting is then said to have two, three, or four chief planes or groupings, which must be well attuned to each other. Each plane may have minor tonal differentiation within itself, but not so much as to blur the distinction between main groupings. An eye for hues of equal brilliance is necessary to the observance of this rule. If tones are not assembled into main groupings or planes, then order, clarity, and vigor of composition are sacrificed. An effect of pictorial surface is achieved

15 Twelve steps of gray from white to black, and the twelve hues of the color circle in matching brilliancies

15

only with organization in planes.
The necessity of sustaining a flat over-all effect is the painter's chief motive for constructing planes. They serve to frustrate and neutralize any undesired depth effects. This control of perspective results from the equating of tonal values to those of the planes. The planes can usually be grouped into foreground, middle ground, and background; but the foreground does not necessarily contain the principal figures; the foreground may be quite vacant, and the main action may take place in the middle ground.

The following paintings will suggest some of the possibilities of light-dark composition: "Lemons, Oranges and Rose" by Francisco de Zurbarán (1598–1664), Florence, Coll. A. Contini-Bonacossi; "Man in Golden Helmet" by Rembrandt (1606–1669), Berlin, Kaiser-Friedrich Museum; "Guitar on Mantelpiece" (1915), by Pablo Picasso.

It may seem strange to identify a sensation of temperature with the visual realm of color sensation. However, experiments have demonstrated a difference of five to seven degrees in the subjective feeling of heat or cold between a workroom painted in blue-green and one painted in red-orange. That is, in the blue-green room the occupants felt that 59° F. was cold, whereas in the red-orange room they did not feel cold until the temperature fell to 52–54° F. Objectively, this meant that blue-green slows down the circulation and red-orange stimulates it.

Similar results were obtained in an animal experiment. A racing stable was divided into two sections, the one painted blue, the other red-orange. In the blue section, horses soon quieted down after running, but in the red section they remained hot and restless for some time. It was found that there were no flies in the blue section, and a great many in the red section.

Both experiments illustrate the pertinence of cold-warm contrast to color planning of interiors. The properties of cold and warm colors are essential to color therapeutics in hospitals.

Going back to the color circle, we have seen that yellow is the lightest and violet the darkest hue; that is, these two hues have the strongest light-dark contrast. At right angles to the yellow-violet axis, we have red-orange versus blue-green, the two poles of cold-warm contrast. Red-orange, or minium, is the warmest, and blue-green, or manganese oxide, is the coldest. Generally the colors yellow, yellow-orange, orange, red-orange, red and red-violet are referred to as warm, and yellow-green, green, blue-green, blue, blue-violet and violet as cold; but this classification can be very misleading. Just as the poles white and black represent the lightest and the darkest color, while all grays are light or dark only relatively, according as they are contrasted with lighter or darker tones, so blue-green and red-orange, the cold and warm poles, are always cold and warm respectively; but the hues intermediate between them in the color circle may be either cold or warm according as they are contrasted with warmer or colder tones.

The cold-warm property can be verbalized in a number of other contrary terms:

cold	warm
shadow	sun
transparent	opaque
sedative	stimulant
rare	dense
airy	earthy
far	near
light	heavy
wet	dry

These diverse impressions illustrate the versatile expressive powers of cold-warm contrast. It can be used to produce highly pictorial effects. In landscape, more distant objects always seem colder in color because of the intervening depth of air.
Cold-warm contrast, then, contains elements suggesting nearness and distance. It is an important medium of representation for plastic and perspective effects.

When a composition is to be done in the pure style of a particular contrast, all other, incidental contrast must be used with restraint, if at all.
In exercises on cold-warm contrast, let us eliminate light-dark contrast entirely; that is, all the colors of a composition are to be equally light or dark.

Fig. 16 illustrates cold-warm contrast in its polar antithesis: red-orange/blue-green.

Fig. 17 inverts the proportions by area.

Figs. 18 and 19 show the same violet; warm at the top, because the adjacent hues are colder, and cold at the bottom, because the adjacent hues are warmer.

Cold-Warm Contrast

16 The strongest cold-warm contrast: red-orange/blue-green
17 Inversion of proportions of Fig. 16
18 Red-violet seems warm relative to blue
19 Red-violet seems cold relative to orange
20 Checkered composition contrasting cold and warm colors
21 Cold-warm modulation in red
22 Cold-warm modulation in green

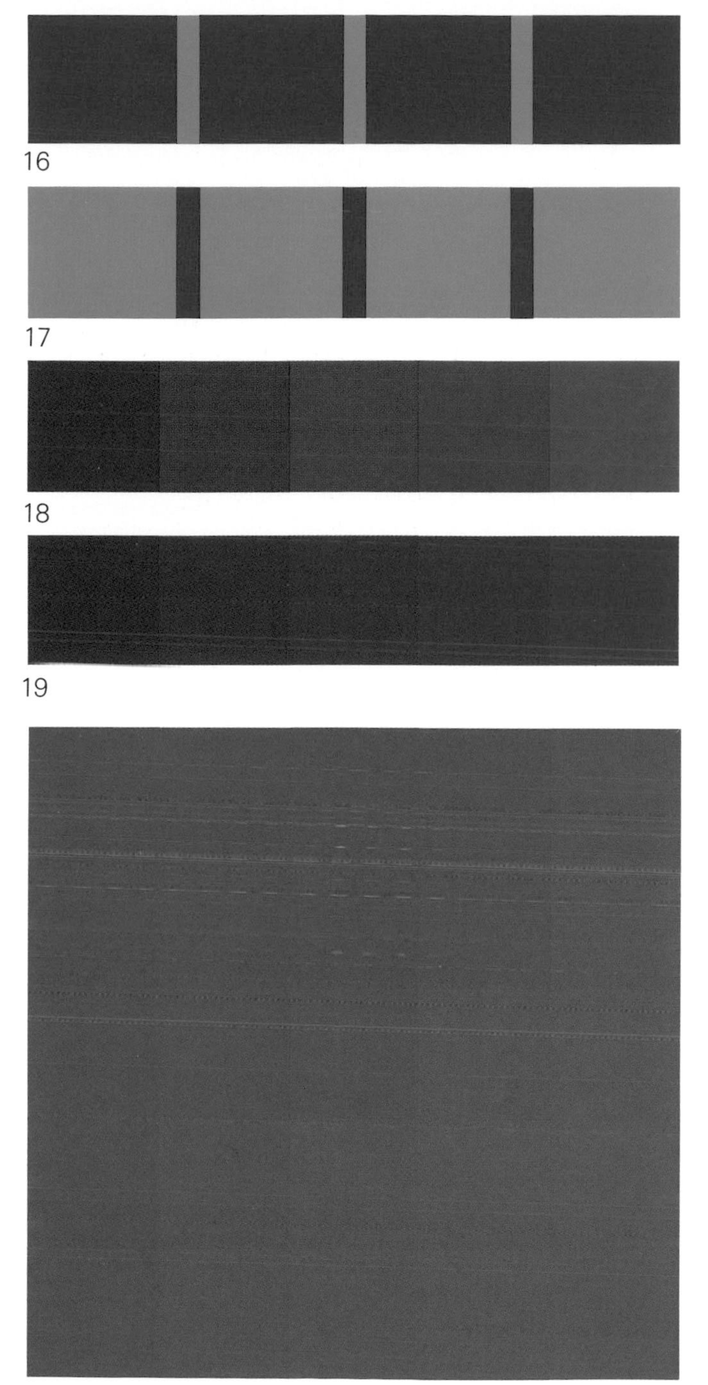
16

17

18

19

21

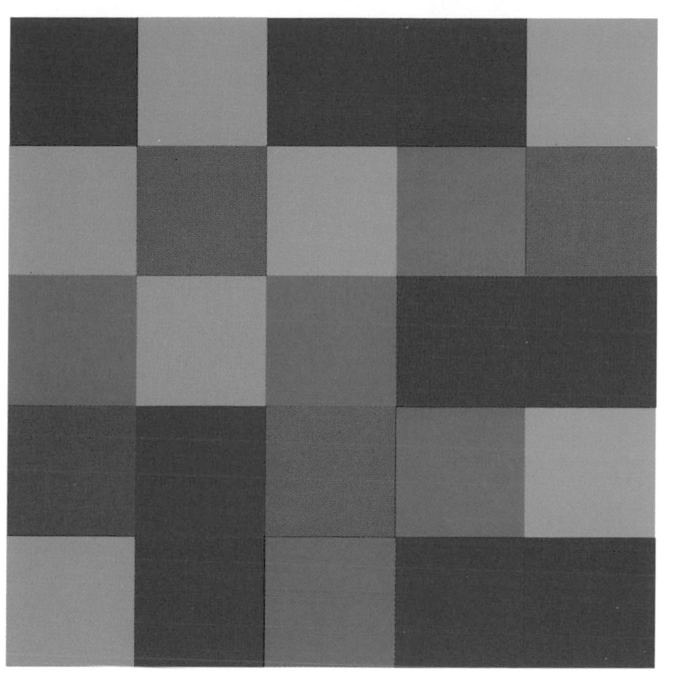
20

22

Fig. 21 shows cold-warm modulations in the range from red to orange.

Fig. 22 shows cold-warm modulations in the range from green to blue-green.

These modulations can be executed at any level of tonality, but a medium brilliance is the most effective.
The variation of hue should go no further than four successive steps of the 12-hue color circle.
An exercise in red-orange, then, may employ orange, yellow-orange, red, and red-violet, in addition to red-orange; and an exercise in blue-green may employ green, yellow-green, blue and blue-violet, in addition to blue-green.
If both poles, the extremes of cold and warm, are to be included, we must form a chromatic scale from blue-green through blue, blue-violet, violet, red-violet and red, to red-orange. This full scale may of course consist of a larger or smaller number of steps. A full chromatic cold-warm scale from blue-green to red-orange by way of yellow is feasible only if all the tones are of the same brilliance as the yellow; otherwise we get light-dark contrast.
These modulations achieve the perfection of their beauty only when light-dark differences are absent.

Whereas Figs. 21 and 22 show chromatic gradations of cold and warm colors, a checkerboard composition heightens the effect by contrast of cold and warm colors (Fig. 20).

Of all the seven color contrasts, the cold-warm contrast is the most sonorous. It provides the possibility of representing the music of the spheres in colors. Grünewald chose this contrast for the color design of his Angel choir, and also for two other parts of the Isenheim altarpiece – the group of angels attendant upon God the Father in the panel of the Madonna, and the painting of the Resurrection. He employed this color effect in portraying the celestial.

When Abbot Suger had the first stained glass windows installed in his Basilica of St. Denis near Paris, he justified his proceeding with the words, "... that the material sense of man may be directed to that which is beyond matter."
These windows were "flashing hieroglyphs," intelligible to all. Their mystic splendor gave the faithful an experience of radiant transcendence. This visual experience was a direct invitation to higher spirituality.
The stained glass window known as "La Belle Verrière" in Chartres Cathedral is composed in a symbolic use of warm red and cold blue. It breathes the same rhythm as the sun. The moving light of heaven continuously changes its incidence, and the sheen of the colors is different at every hour of the day. The translucent glass has a radiance like that of precious stones.

When Monet began to devote himself to landscape, he ceased to paint in the studio, and worked out-of-doors. He made intensive studies of seasons, times of day, and weather conditions, with their changing light and mood. He meant to portray the shimmer of light in the air and over warm fields, color refractions in cloud and mist, highlights of flowing, undulant water, and the alternation of sunny and shady green in the foliage of trees. He observed that light and shade, and rainbow reflections from all sides, resolved the local colors of objects into elements of cold and warm rather than light and dark variation. In his landscapes, the light-dark contrast emphasized by earlier painting is superseded in importance by cold-warm contrast.

The Impressionists noticed that the cold, transparent blue of the sky and atmosphere was everywhere in contrast, as a shadow color, with the warm tones of sunlight. The enchantment of Monet's, Pissarro's and Renoir's paintings is often achieved by the cunning play of modulations of cold and warm colors.

We call two colors complementary if their pigments, mixed together, yield a neutral gray-black. Physically, light of two complementary colors, mixed together, will yield white.
Two such colors make a strange pair. They are opposite, they require each other. They incite each other to maximum vividness when adjacent; and they annihilate each other, to gray-black, when mixed – like fire and water.

There is always but one color complementary to a given color. In the color circle, Fig. 3, complementary colors are diametrically opposite each other.
Examples of complementary pairs are:

yellow, violet
blue, orange
red, green

If we analyze these pairs of complementaries, we find that all three primaries – yellow, red, blue – are always present:

yellow, violet = yellow, red + blue
blue, orange = blue, yellow + red
red, green = red, yellow + blue

Just as the mixture of yellow, red, and blue is a gray-black, so the mixture of any two complementaries is gray-black.
We also recall the experiment showing that if one hue of the spectrum is suppressed, all the others mixed together will yield its complementary. For every hue, the sum of all the other colors in the spectrum is the complementary of that hue.
Both the phenomenon of afterimage and the effects of simultaneity illustrate the remarkable physiological fact, as yet unexplained, that the eye requires any given color to be balanced by the complementary, and will spontaneously generate the latter if it is not present. This principle is of great importance in all practical work with color. In the section on concord of colors, we stated that the rule of complementaries is the basis of harmonious design because its observance establishes a precise equilibrium in the eye.

Complementary colors, used in the proper proportions, give the effect of a statically fixed image. Each color stands unmodified in its intensity. Here the agent coincides with the effect. This stabilizing power of complementary colors is especially important in mural painting.
Each complementary pair has its own peculiarities.
Thus, yellow/violet represents not only complementary contrast but also an extreme light-dark contrast.
Red-orange/blue-green is a complementary pair, and at the same time the extreme of cold-warm contrast.
Red and green are complementary, and the two saturated colors have the same brilliance.

Some exercises will help illustrate the nature of complementary contrast.

Figs. 23–28 show six complementary pairs and their

mixtures towards gray. These scales are prepared by adding more and more of the complementary to a given color. In the center of each series, we get a gray. If the mixtures of two colors in all proportions fail to include a neutral gray, it follows that the two colors are not complementary.

Fig. 29 is a composition in a pair of complementaries and modulations of their mixtures. Instead, of course, two, three, or more pairs of complementaries can be used. Fig. 30 shows a square array of mixtures of the complementary pairs orange/blue and red-orange/blue-green.

Many paintings based on complementary contrast exhibit not only the contrasting complementaries themselves but also their graduated mixtures as intermediates and compensating tones. Being related to the pure colors, they unite the two into one family. In fact, these mixed tones often occupy more space than the pure colors.

Nature shows such mixed colors very elegantly. They are to be seen in the stems and leaves of a red rosebush before the blossoms appear. The red of the unblown rose mixes with the green of stem and leaf to lovely red-gray and green-gray nuances.

Two complementary colors can be used to make beautiful chromatic grays. The Old Masters produced such grays by the technique of striping a pure color with coats of the complementary, or by varnishing the first with a thin film of the second. Pointillism produces chromatic grays in still another way. The pure colors are laid side-by-side in tiny dots, and the mixing operation is performed visually in the eye.

These paintings exemplify the use of complementary contrast: "Madonna of the Chancellor Rolin" by Jan van Eyck (1390–1441), Paris, the Louvre; "Solomon Receiving the Queen of Sheba," by Piero della Francesca (1410/11–1492), from a mural at Arezzo; "La Montagne Sainte-Victoire" by Paul Cézanne (1839–1906), Philadelphia Museum of Art.

Complementary Contrast

23–28 Mixture bands of six complementary pairs

29 Composition in the complementary pair red/green and mixtures

30 Mixture square of two complementary pairs, orange/blue and red-orange/blue-green

23

24

25

26

27

28

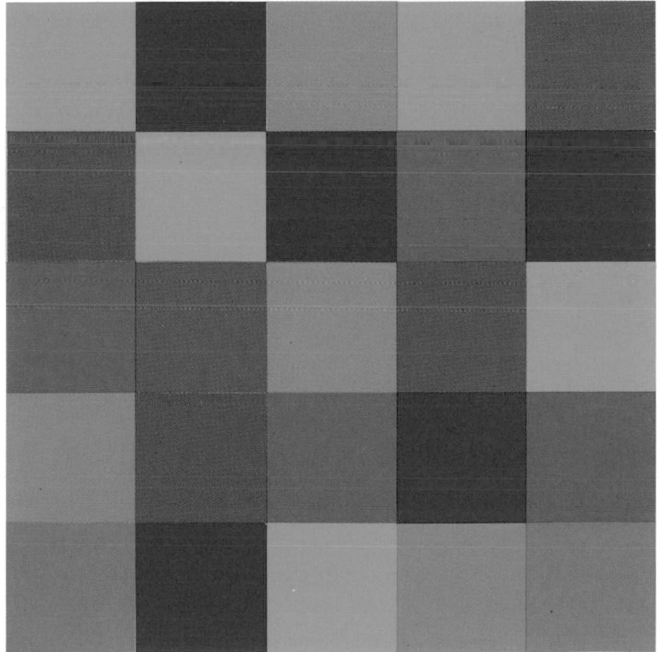
29

30

Simultaneous contrast results from the fact that for any given color the eye simultaneously requires the complementary color, and generates it spontaneously if it is not already present. By virtue of this fact, the fundamental principle of color harmony implies the rule of complementaries.
The simultaneously generated complementary occurs as a sensation in the eye of the beholder, and is not objectively present. It cannot be photographed. Simultaneous contrast may with reason be placed on a par with successive contrast.

One may make the following experiment: On a large, strongly colored area, examine a small black square, first laying a sheet of tissue paper on top. If the area is red, the black square will look greenish gray; if green, then reddish; if violet, then yellowish; if yellow, then the black square will look violet-gray. Each hue simultaneously generates its complementary.
Figs. 31–36 illustrate this experiment in another form. In each of the six pure colors, I place a small neutral gray square, exactly matching the surrounding color in brilliance. Each of the small squares is tinged, for the eye, with the complementary to the background hue.

Simultaneous Contrast

31–36 Each of six pure color squares contains a small neutral gray square, matching the background color in brilliance. Each gray square seems to be tinged with the complementary of the background. The simultaneous effect becomes more intense, the longer the principal color of a square is viewed

37 Three small gray squares, surrounded by orange. Three grays barely distinct from each other have been used. The first gray is bluish, and intensifies the simultaneous effect; the second gray is neutral, and suffers simultaneous modification; the third gray contains an admixture of orange, and therefore fails to be modified

31

32

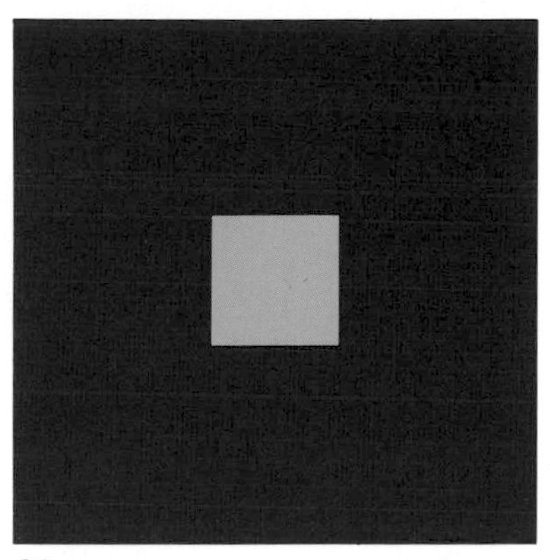

33

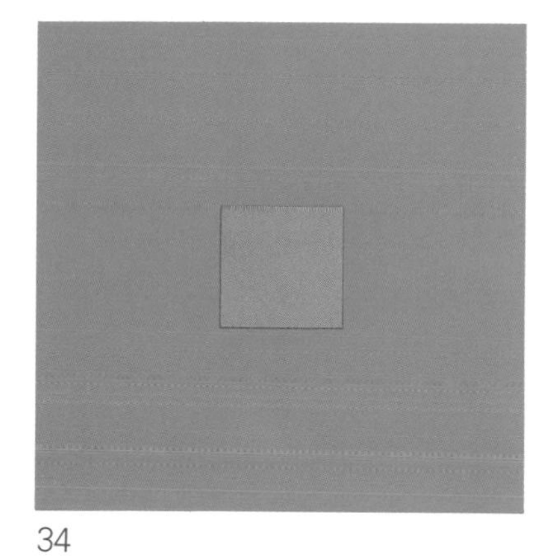

34

35

36

37

When gazing at one of the colors, it is best to hide the others and hold the page not too far from the eyes.
Simultaneous effects become more intense, the longer the background is viewed and the more luminous the color. The effect is intensified if the background is lighted from in front and the example placed slightly below eye level, so that the whole is viewed in obliquely incident light.
The simultaneously appearing color, not being objectively present but generated in the eye, induces a feeling of excitement and lively vibration of everchanging intensity. Under sustained viewing, the given color seems to lose intensity, as the eye tires, while the sensation of the simultaneous hue grows stronger.
The simultaneous effect occurs not only between a gray and a strong chromatic color, but also between any two colors that are not precisely complementary. Each of the two will tend to shift the other towards its own complement, and generally both will lose some of their intrinsic character and become tinged with new effects. Under these conditions, colors give an appearance of dynamic activity. Their stability is disturbed, and they are set in changeable oscillation. They lose their objective character and move in an individual field of action of an unreal kind, as if in a new dimension. Color is as if dematerialized. The principle that the agent of a color sensation does not always agree with its effect is fully operative.

Simultaneous effect is of paramount importance to all who are concerned with color. Goethe said that simultaneous contrast determines the aesthetic utility of color.
In Fig. 37 there are three small gray squares in an orange field. Three just perceptibly different grays have been used. The unlike effects of the three different grays are due to the fact that a little blue has been mixed with the first gray, and this cooperates with the simultaneous effect; the second gray is neutral, and shows the simultaneous effect alone; while the third gray contains an admixture of orange just sufficient to cancel the simultaneous effect, and therefore shows no simultaneous modification. This experiment clearly shows how the exciting effect of simultaneous contrast can be amplified or suppressed by suitable devices.
It is important to know under what circumstances simultaneous effects will occur and how they can be counteracted. There are many problems in color that preclude solutions using simultaneous contrast. Some years ago, the manager of a weaving mill called my attention, in desperation, to some hundreds of meters of costly tie silk that would not sell because a black stripe on a red ground looked, not black, but green. This effect was so pronounced that customers insisted that the yarn was green. If brownish black yarn had been used, the simultaneous effect would have been neutralized, and heavy losses avoided.
In addition to this means of avoiding the effect of simultaneous contrast, there is another possibility; the susceptible hues may be used in unlike brilliance. Once a light-dark contrast is present, simultaneous influences are diminished.
Simultaneous effects occur among pure colors when a complementary hue is replaced by its right- or left-hand neighbor in the 12-hue color circle. For violet, for example, in opposition to yellow, we substitute red-violet or blue-violet. Effects of simultaneous contrast can be intensified with the aid of contrast of extension.
It is always advisable to juxtapose the hues to be employed in a composition, using a preliminary sketch to check color effects, before proceeding to execution.

The following paintings may be cited as examples of the use of simultaneous contrast: "Satan and the Locusts", from the "Apocalypse de St. Sever" (11th century), Paris, Bibliothèque Nationale; "Stripping of Christ" by El Greco (1541–1614), Munich, Pinakothek; "Café at Evening" by Vincent van Gogh (1853–1890), Otterloo, Rijksmuseum Kröller-Müller.

Saturation, or quality, relates to the degree of purity of a color. Contrast of saturation is the contrast between pure, intense colors and dull, diluted colors. The prismatic hues produced by dispersion of white light are colors of maximum saturation or intensity of hue.
We have colors of maximum saturation among pigments also. We recall the curve pointed out in Fig. 15, connecting pigmentary colors of highest purity and intensity.
Colors may be diluted in four different ways, with very different results.

1) A pure color may be diluted with white. This renders its character somewhat colder. Carmine assumes a bluish cast as it is mixed with white, and becomes sharply altered in character. Yellow is cooled by white; the character of blue is hardly changed. Violet is extremely sensitive to white. Whereas saturated dark violet has something menacing about it, violet lightened with white – lilac – has an agreeable and quietly cheerful effect.

2) A color may be diluted with black. This admixture deprives yellow of its brilliant character, turning it into something sickly or insidiously poisonous. Its splendor is gone. Géricault's picture "Les Aliénés" is in black-yellow, and has an overwhelming expression of mental derangement.
Violet is enhanced by black in its "inherent" gloom, fading as it were into night.
By admixture of black, carmine acquires a timbre in the direction of violet.
Vermilion diluted with black gives a kind of burnt, red-brown pigment.
Blue is eclipsed by black. It will suffer only a few degrees of dilution before its light is extinguished.
Green admits of far more modulation than violet or blue, and has many possible alterations.
Quite in general, black deprives colors of their quality

of light. It alienates them from light, and sooner or later deadens them.

3) A saturated color can be diluted by mixing it with white and black, or in other words with gray. As soon as I mix gray with a saturated color, I get tones which may be of equal, greater or less brightness, but in any case less intense than the corresponding pure color. Admixture of gray renders colors more or less dull and neutral.
Delacroix hated gray in a painting, and avoided it as much as possible. Mixed grays are easily neutralized by simultaneous contrast effects.

4) Pure colors may be diluted by admixture of the corresponding complementary colors. If I add yellow to violet, I get tones intermediate between the light yellow and the dark violet. Green and red are not much different in tonality, but when mixed they descend into gray-black. The various mixtures of two complementary colors lightened with white produce rare tints.

Contrast of Saturation

38–41 On a checkered pattern of 25 squares, luminous yellow, orange, red, or blue is placed in the center. The four corners are neutral gray in the same brilliance as the pure color. Graded admixture of gray with the pure color produces intermediate shades of low saturation

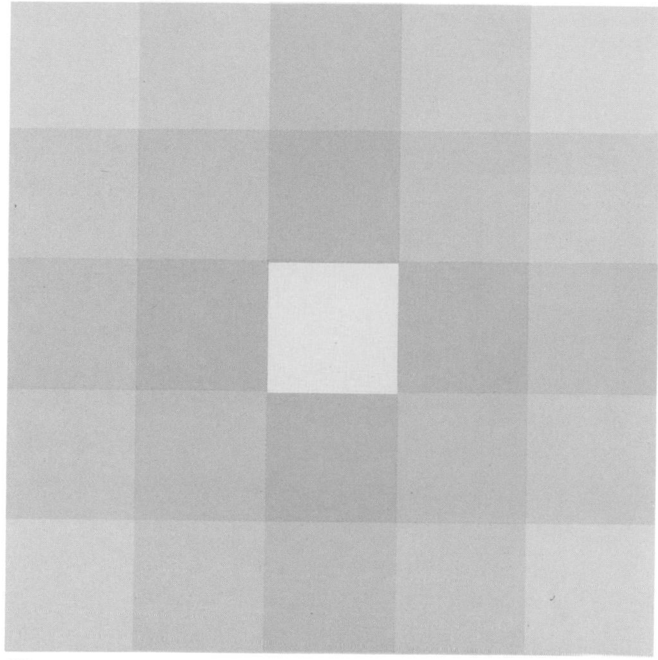
38

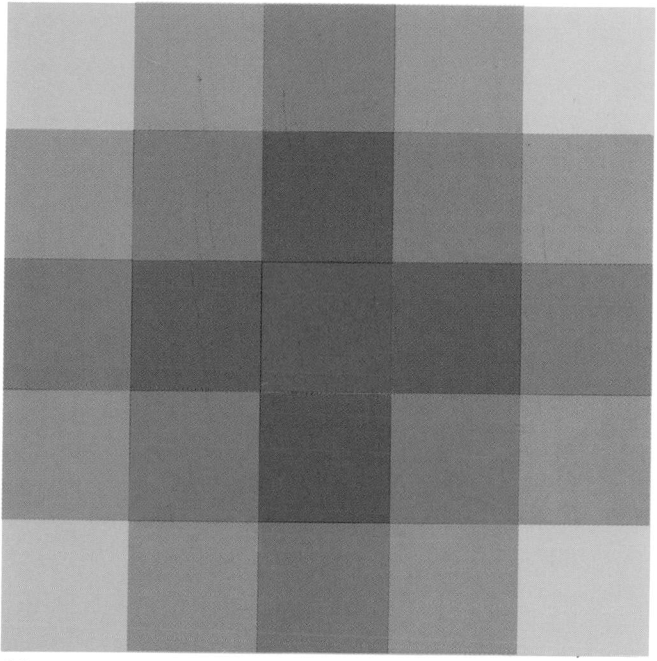
39

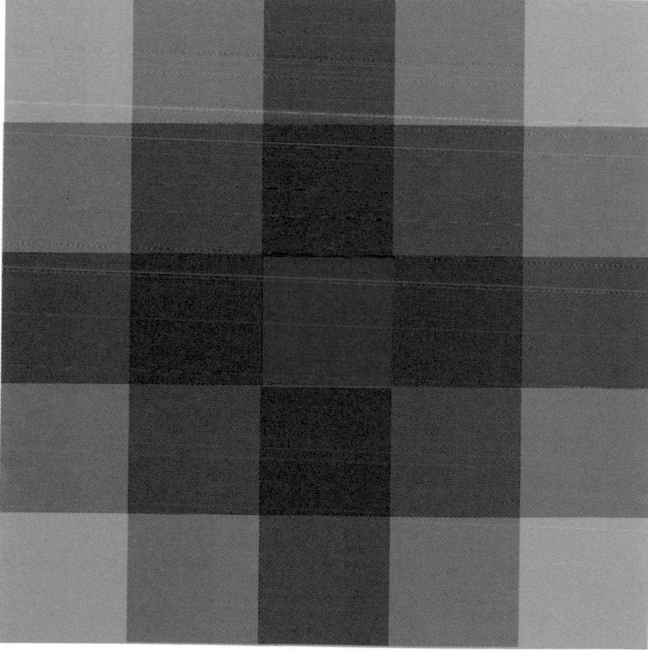
40

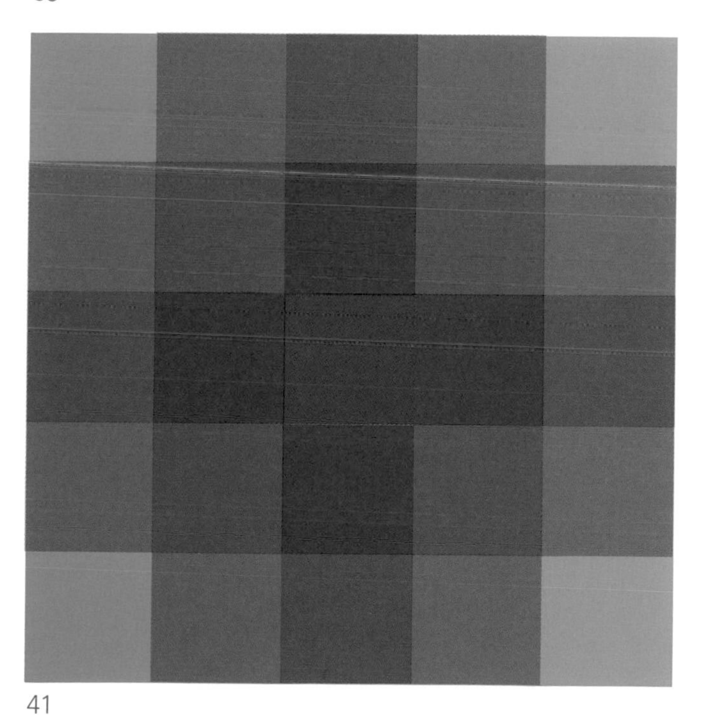
41

When a mixture contains all three primaries, the resulting hue assumes a dim, diluted character. Depending on the proportions, it will appear yellowish, reddish or bluish gray or black. All degrees of dilution can be obtained with the three primaries. The same applies to the three secondaries, or to any other combination provided only that yellow, red, and blue are all present in the total mixture.
The effect of ''dull-vivid'' contrast is relative. A color may appear vivid beside a dull tone, and dull beside a more vivid tone.

Basic exercises in contrast of saturation can be performed on a checkerboard of twenty-five squares. We place a pure color in the center, and a neutral gray of the same brilliance in each of the four corners. We then mix gray with the pure color step-by-step, obtaining four more or less diluted intermediates. To comprehend contrast of saturation, we must eliminate light-dark contrast; hence the brilliances of all squares must be the same. The exercises of Figs. 38–41 show the delicate character of this contrast in its chromatic modulations. Similar exercises can be done by placing the complementary of the central color in the corner squares, instead of gray. In such an exercise, the effect will be more colorful than in the one found here.

If we wish to express pure contrast of saturation in a composition, without any other contrast, then the dull color must be mixed from the same hue as the intense one; that is, intense red must contrast with dull red, and intense blue with dull blue.
Otherwise, the pure contrast would be drowned out by other contrasts, such as cold-warm contrast, impairing the quiet and restful effect.

Dull tones, most especially grays, live by virtue of the vivid ones surrounding them. This may be observed by dividing an area checkerboard-fashion and placing a neutral gray in every other square, with vivid colors of the same brilliance as the gray in the remaining squares. The gray will be seen to take on vividness, while the surrounding chromatic colors appear reduced and comparatively weakened.

The use of contrast of quality is well seen in the following paintings for example: ''Newborn Babe'' by Georges de La Tour (d. 1659), Musée de Rennes; ''Le Piano'' by Henri Matisse (1859–1954), New York, Museum of Modern Art; ''Magic Fish'' by Paul Klee (1879–1940), Philadelphia Museum of Art.

Contrast of extension involves the relative areas of two or more color patches. It is the contrast between much and little, or great and small.

Colors may be assembled in areas of any size. But we should inquire what quantitative proportion between two or more colors may be said to be in balance, with no one of the colors used more prominently than another.
Two factors determine the force of a pure color, its brilliance and its extent. To estimate brilliance or light value, we must compare the pure colors on a neutral-gray background of medium brilliance. We find that the intensities or light values of the several hues are different.
Goethe set up simple numerical ratios for these values, best suited to our purpose. They are approximate, but who would demand precise data when commercial pigments sold under the same name can vary so widely? Ultimately, vision must decide. Furthermore, the color areas in a painting are often fragmentary and complicated in shape, and it would be difficult to reduce them to simple numerical proportions. The eye is trustworthy enough, provided it be properly sensitized.

Goethe's light values are as follows:

yellow	:	orange	:	red	:	violet	:	blue	:	green
9	:	8	:	6	:	3	:	4	:	6

The proportionalities for complementary pairs are:

yellow : violet $= 9 : 3 = 3 : 1 = \frac{3}{4} : \frac{1}{4}$
orange : blue $= 8 : 4 = 2 : 1 = \frac{2}{3} : \frac{1}{3}$
red : green $= 6 : 6 = 1 : 1 = \frac{1}{2} : \frac{1}{2}$

In converting these values to harmonious areas, I must take the reciprocals of the light values; that is, yellow, being three times as strong, must occupy only one-third as much area as its complementary violet.

As Figs. 42–44 illustrate, we obtain the following harmonious relative areas for the complementaries:

yellow : violet $= \frac{1}{4} : \frac{3}{4}$
orange : blue $= \frac{1}{3} : \frac{2}{3}$
red : green $= \frac{1}{2} : \frac{1}{2}$

The harmonious areas for the primary and secondary colors are therefore as follows:

yellow	:	orange	:	red	:	violet	:	blue	:	green
3	:	4	:	6	:	9	:	8	:	6

Or:

yellow : orange = 3 : 4
yellow : red = 3 : 6
yellow : violet = 3 : 9
yellow : blue = 3 : 8
yellow : red : blue = 3 : 6 : 8
orange : violet : green = 4 : 9 : 6

– and so forth; all the other colors are to be related to each other similarly.

Contrast of Extension

42–44 Harmonious proportions of area for complementary colors:
Yellow : Violet $= \frac{1}{4} : \frac{3}{4}$
Orange : Blue $= \frac{1}{3} : \frac{2}{3}$
Red : Green $= \frac{1}{2} : \frac{1}{2}$

45 Circle of primary and secondary colors in harmonious proportion

46 Equal proportions of red and green

47 A little red with a great deal of green makes the red highly active

42

43

44

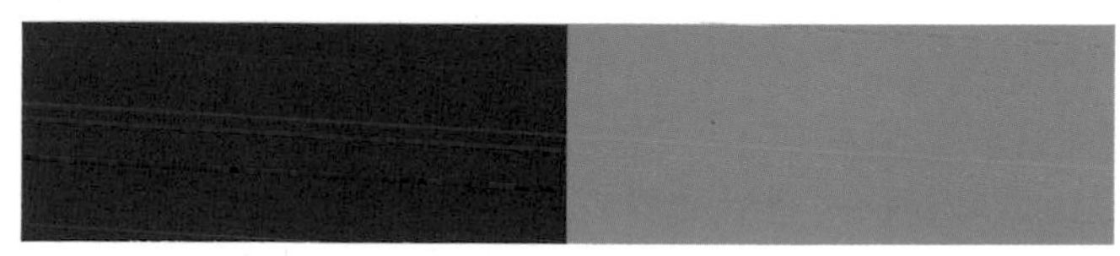

45

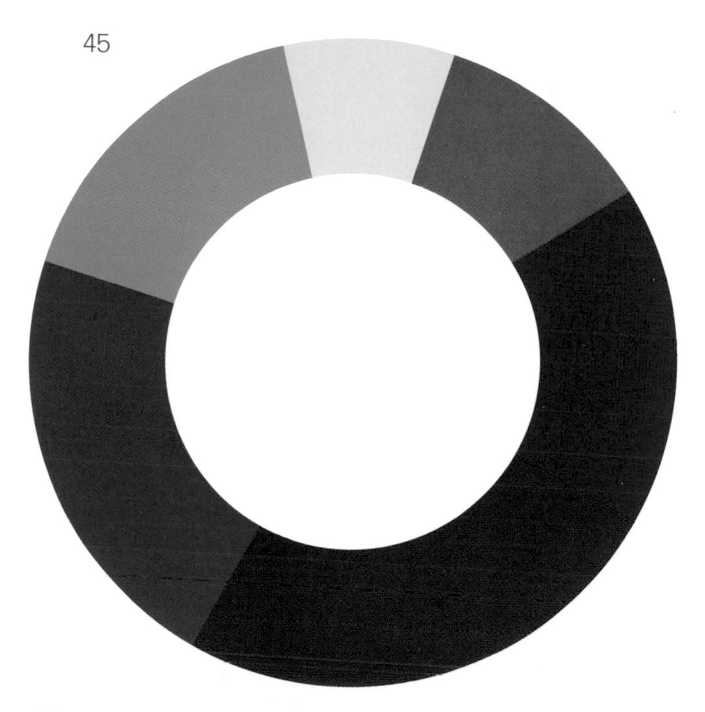

46

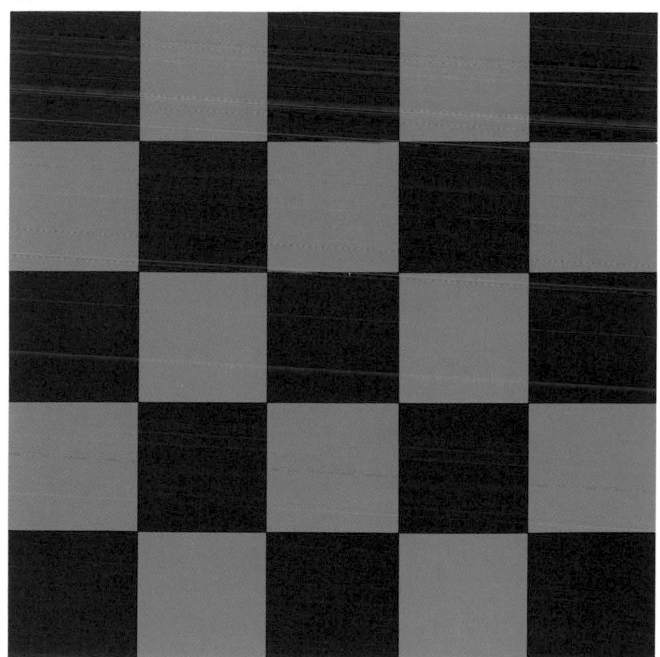

47

Fig. 45 shows the primary and secondary color circle of harmonious extension. This is constructed as follows: First, a whole circle is divided into three equal parts and each third is in turn divided in the proportions for two complementary colors.

One third of the circle is divided for
yellow : violet :: ¼ : ¾
Another third is divided for
orange : blue :: ⅓ : ⅔ and
The last third is divided for
red : green :: ½ : ½

When all these arcs have been found, another equal circle is drawn, and the sectors are transferred in the sequence of the prismatic color circle, namely yellow, orange, red, violet, blue, green.
Harmonic areas yield static, quiet effects. Contrast of extension is neutralized when the harmonious proportions are used.
The ratios here stated are valid only when all the hues appear in their maximum purity. If these are altered, the equilibrium areas also change. The two factors of light value and extent of area turn out to be most intimately related.
If other than harmonious proportions are used in a color composition, thus allowing one color to dominate, then the effect obtained is expressive. What proportions are to be chosen in an expressive composition depends on subject matter, artistic sense, and personal taste.

What effect is obtained when contrast of extension is very pronounced? In Fig. 47, red is scantily represented. Because green is present in large quantity compared to red, it simultaneously generates an exciting luminosity of its complementary red in the eye. It was stated in the section on simultaneous contrast that the eye demands the complement to a given hue. It is not yet known why this is so. Perhaps we are ruled by some universal will to compensation or counterassertion. Contrast of extension owes its special effect to a similar tendency. The minority color, in distress, as it were, reacts defensively to seem relatively more vivid than if, as in Fig. 46, it were present in a harmonious amount. A similar law of compensation is seen to operate in biology. In plants or animals, under adverse conditions of life, there is a mobilization of powers of resistance, expressing itself in heightened performance, given the opportunity. If a color present in minute amount is given opportunity, by protracted contemplation, to assert itself in the eye, it is found to become increasingly concentrated and provocative.

The use of two mutually intensified contrasts can produce very live and strange color expressions.

A special property of contrast of extension is here exemplified; it is capable of modifying and intensifying the effect of any other contrast. Mention was made of proportion under the heading of light-dark contrast. Contrast of extension is, properly speaking, a contrast of proportion. In light-dark composition, if a small bright spot contrasts with a large area of darkness, this antithesis may lend the picture an enlarged and deepened significance.

Attention to the color areas in composition is at least as important as the actual choice of colors. Any color composition should be evolved from the relationships of elements of area to each other.

Color areas should take their form, extent, and outline from chroma and intensity of color, and not be predetermined by delineation.

Observance of this rule is particularly important to the proper determination of color extensions. The correct sizes of color areas are not to be laid out by means of outline, since the proportions are governed by the chromatic forces evolving out of hue, saturation, brilliance,

and contrast effects.
A yellow area that is to hold its place among light tints must be of a different size than an area of the same yellow against dark shades. The tints call for a large yellow area; among shades, a small yellow area is enough to allow the brilliance of the hue to operate. Proportions of all color areas should be similarly derived from their relative potentials.
As an example of the contrast of extension, we may mention the painting "Landscape with Fall of Icarus" by Pieter Brueghel the Elder (1520–1569), Brussels, Musées Royaux des Beaux Arts.

To acquaint ourselves further with the kingdom of color, let us list some exercises in systematic mixing.
According to the sensitivity and technique at our command, we may choose few or many intermediate degrees in the various exercises. Any color may be mixed with black, white, or gray; and any color may be mixed with any other color.
The innumerable possible mixtures constitute the copious variety of this universe.

1. Mixture Bands
We place any two colors at the ends of a strip, and prepare graduated mixtures of the two. Depending on the two colors with which we begin, we obtain some scale of mixed tone. These may be varied into tints or shades.

2. Mixture Triangles
We divide each side of an equilateral triangle into three equal parts and join the points of division by lines parallel to the sides of the triangle. This makes nine small triangles. In the corner triangle, we place yellow, red, and blue, and we mix yellow with red, yellow with blue, and red with blue, for the triangles midway between the corners. In each of the remaining triangles, we place the mixture of the three colors adjoining it. The same thing can be done starting with other colors.

3. Mixture Squares
When, as starting points, we place white, black, and the pair of complementaries red and green in the corners of a square divided into 25 small squares, we next paint in the mixtures between the given colors along the edges, and then the progressions along the diagonals; and finally we chromatically interpolate the missing tones.
Instead of black, white, red and green, two pairs of complementaries may be used as in Fig. 29, or any colors may be chosen.
The tones of a mixture triangle or square form a complete family, all interrelated.

Anyone wishing to explore further the possibilities of color mixing should try mixing each hue with each of the others. Rule off a large square into 13 by 13 small squares. The first space at the upper left is kept white. The remaining squares of the top row are filled in with the twelve hues of the color circle from yellow through yellow-orange to yellow-green. The remaining squares of the left-hand column are filled in with the same hues in complementary sequence, from violet through blue-violet and blue to red-violet. The second row is completed by mixing each hue of the first row with violet. In the third row, each hue of the first row is mixed with blue-violet. When each hue of the left-hand column has been mixed with each hue of the top row, then the large square will show a diagonal of grays from upper left to lower right, where the complementaries meet.

El Greco, Rembrandt, Cézanne, and other masters

produced remarkable mixtures by overlaying transparent pigments. Seurat and the Neo-Impressionists instead placed pure hues side-by-side, to form additive mixtures in the eye of the beholder.

When the student has completed a number of exercises in mixing colors, he may proceed to reproduce given tones as accurately as possible by mixing. Models may be taken from nature, works of art, or any other source. I think the value of such practice lies in improved perception of colors and verification of that perception by precise reproduction. Just as in the most delicate industrial processes, measurement and calculation ultimately break down, and the right result can be obtained only through the skill of the specially endowed craftsman, so the artistically decisive mixtures and compositions of colors can be perfected only through color sense.

Generally speaking, sensitivity to color is biased in the same way as subjective taste. Persons of a blue subjective timbre will perceive numerous variations of blue, but possibly very few of red. It is therefore worth while to carry the exercises through the whole domain of colors. In this way we become more just in our evaluation of all colors.

Besides the pigmentary method of color mixing thus far discussed, there is also the method of visual mixing. This consists in juxtaposing the pure colors to be mixed in small areas or dots, and then viewing the resulting dotted surface, or pointillé, from some distance. In the eye, the dots are mixed into a unitary color sensation. The advantage of this additive kind of mixing is that the resulting tones are less diluted and more vibrant.

The same breakdown of color areas into elementary dots is employed in color printing. The eye unites the dots into continuous areas. When the reproduction is viewed through a magnifier, the minute dots of color can be seen individually. In ordinary four-color printing, the many different shadings are produced by combinations or mixtures of four standardized colors: yellow, blue-green, bluish red, and black. Obviously, these four components and their mixtures will not always yield the utmost fidelity of reproduction. When extremely high quality of rendition is to be achieved, seven or more color plates are used.

Another everyday example of subjective color mixing is to be found in weaving. Differently colored warp and woof threads combine, according to the weave, into a more or less integrated field. A familiar pattern is that of the Scottish plaids. Where a set of colored warp threads intersects a group of weft threads of the same hue, squares of pure vivid color occur. Where the intersecting threads are of unlike hue, the warp and weft colors are mixed; the area actually consists of differently colored dots, but it looks homogeneous at some distance. The original tartan patterns, woven in fine wool, were the heraldic property of particular clans. The proportions and coloring of genuine tartans are models of textile design to the present day.

As an example in painting, let me mention Georges Seurat's preliminary study "Un Dimanche à la Grande Jatte" (New York, Metropolitan Museum). In it, the several color patches are dissected into vibrant modulations of contrasting hues. In other words, they are not painted in uniform mixed colors; each patch consists of many different hues, to be united as solid areas only in the eye of the beholder.

Having given an account of the potential effects of colors in their seven contrasts, I shall attempt to provide a clear and complete map of the world of color. In Fig. 3, we developed a 12-hue color circle from the three primaries yellow, red, blue. However, this circular array is not adequate for a complete classification. Instead of a circle, we shall need a sphere, the solid adopted by Philipp Otto Runge as the most convenient for plotting the characteristic and manifold properties of the color universe. The sphere is the elementary shape of universal symmetry. It serves to visualize the rule of complementaries, illustrates all fundamental relationships among colors, and between chromatic colors and black and white. If we imagine the color sphere to be a transparent body, each point within which corresponds to a particular value, then all conceivable colors have a place.

Each point on the sphere can be located by its meridian and parallel. For an adequate color classification, we require only six parallels and 12 meridians.

The Color Sphere

48 Twelve-pointed color star: Each pure color is tinted in two steps to white and shaded in two steps to black

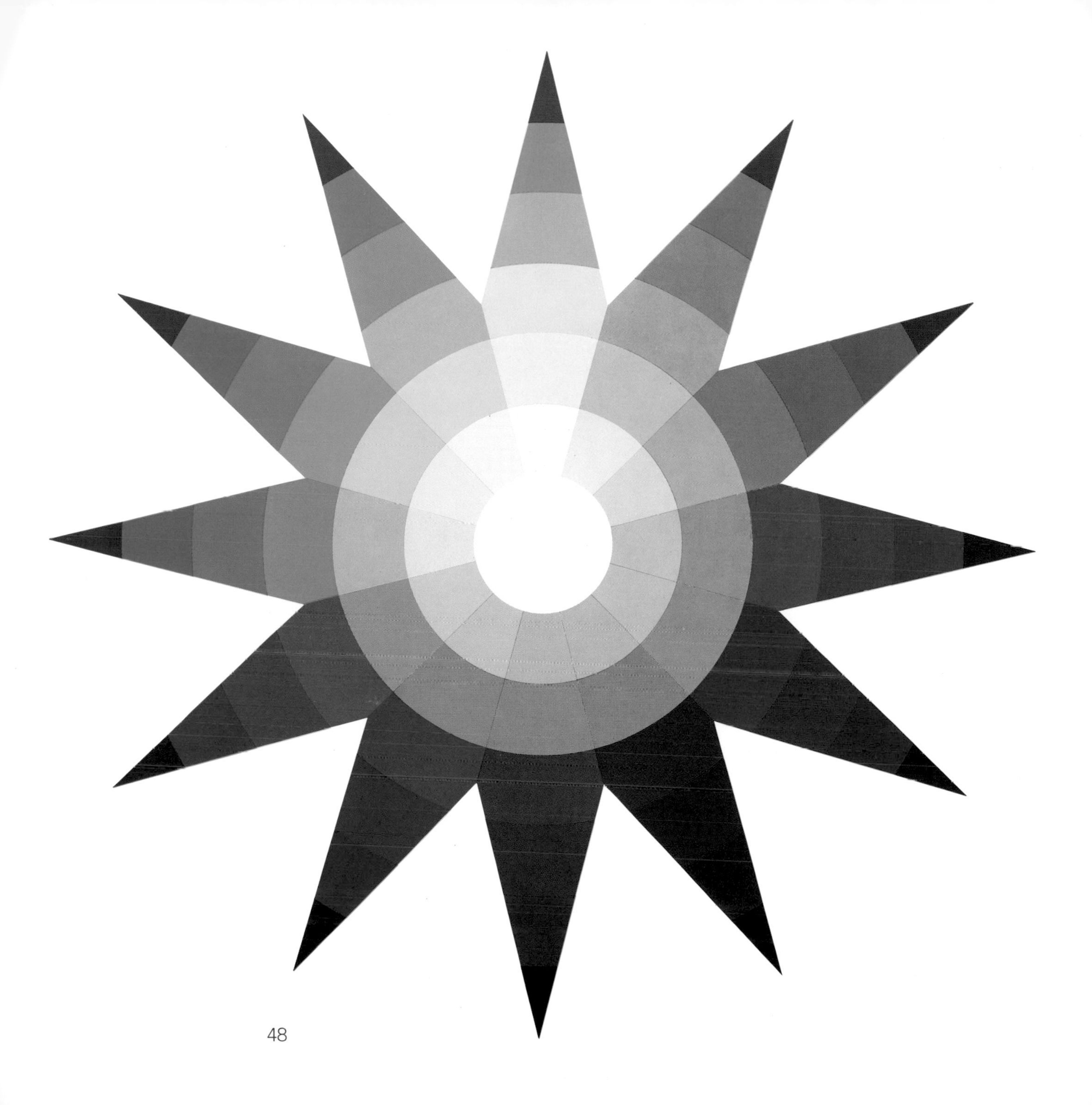

On the surface of the sphere, we draw six equally spaced parallel circles, forming seven zones. Perpendicular to these zones, we draw 12 meridians from pole to pole. On the equatorial zone, in the 12 uniform quadrilaterals obtained, we place the pure colors of our 12-hue color circle. The two polar zones are occupied by white at the top and black at the bottom. In the two zones between white and the equatorial zone, we interpolate two evenly spaced tints of each hue. Between the equatorial zone and the black zone, we interpolate two evenly spaced shades of each hue. Since the 12 pure colors have unequal brilliances, the degrees towards white and black must be adjusted for each color separately. The pure color yellow is very light; and its two tints are therefore close together, whereas its two degrees of shade are far apart. Violet is the darkest of the pure colors, and its tints are widely spaced, whereas its shades are close together. Each of the 12 hues must be lightened and darkened beginning from its normal brilliance, so that we have two zones of tints and two zones of shades of the 12 hues, in each of which zones the tonality varies. Thus the yellow in the zone of first tints is lighter than the violet in that zone. The zones are not belts of uniform brilliance of the twelve hues.

Since we cannot reproduce the color sphere in three dimensions here, we project the spherical surface on a plane. If we view the color sphere from above, we see the white zone in the center, then the two zones of tints, and then half of the equatorial zone of pure colors. Viewing the sphere from below, we have the black zone in the center, then the two zones of shades, and then the other half of the equatorial zone.

In order to see the entire surface of the sphere at once, we may imagine the darker hemisphere to be slit at the meridians and developed in the same plane as the lighter hemisphere. The result is the 12-pointed star of Fig. 48. White is in the center. Reading outward, we have the zones of tints, the zone of the pure hues, and the two zones of shades, with black at the extreme points of the star.

49–50 View of surface of sphere

51 Horizontal section of color sphere at the equator

52 Vertical section of color sphere in the red-orange/blue-green sector

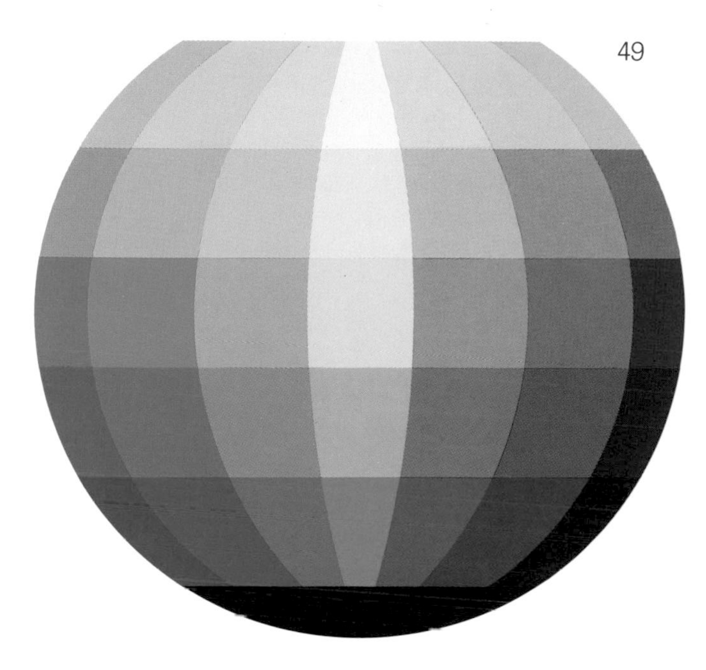

49

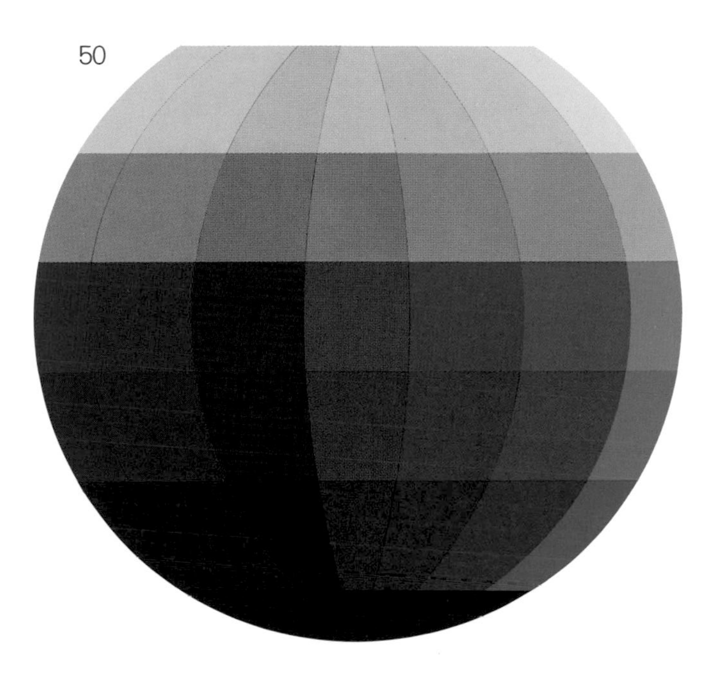

50

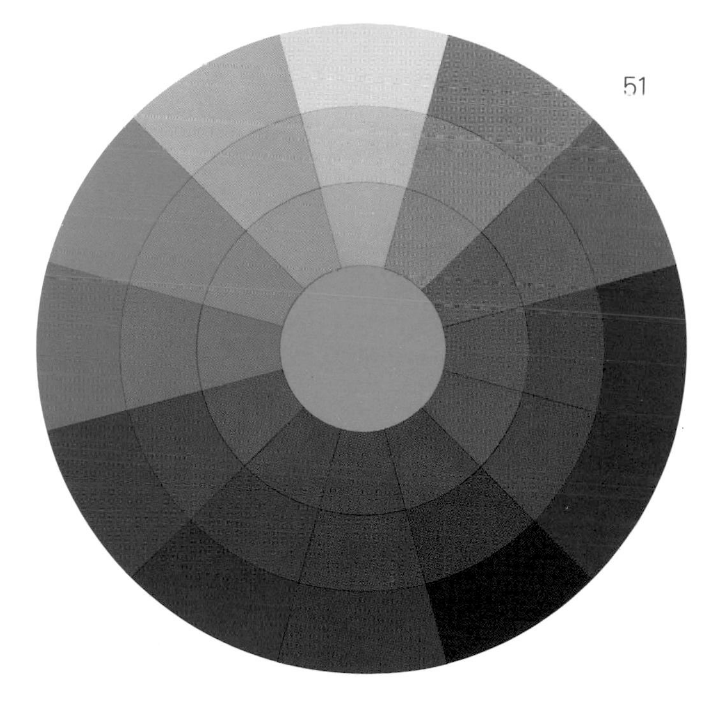

51

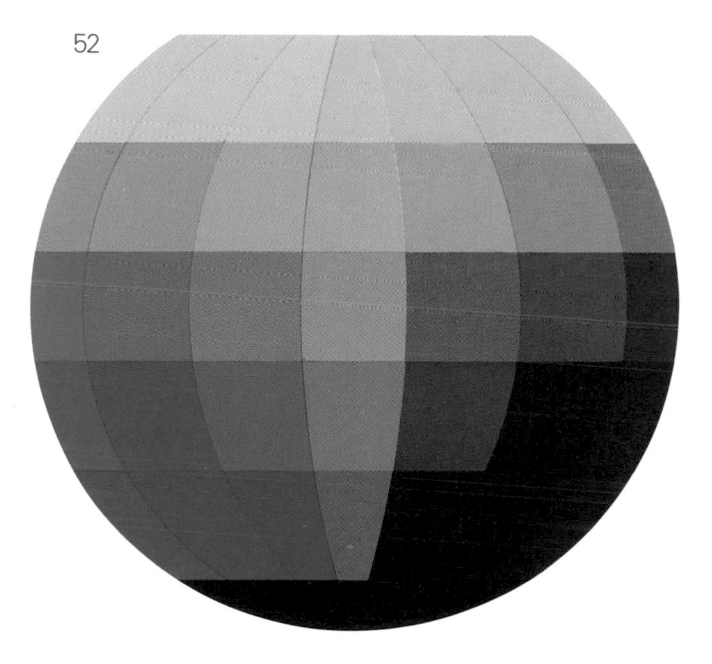

52

Fig. 49 shows an equatorial view of the color sphere. The equatorial zone contains the pure colors, lightened with white in two degrees of brilliance towards the white pole. Towards the black pole, the pure colors are shaded with black in two degrees of darkness. In the same way, Fig. 50 shows the sphere viewed from the other side. So we have taken in the whole surface of the sphere.

In order to find out what is going on inside the sphere, we must take sections.

Fig. 51 shows a horizontal section of the color sphere at the equator. We note the neutral gray region in the center, and the ring of pure hues on the outside. The two strata between the pure colors and the gray are the mixed tones of the corresponding complementary colors.

Such a cross section might of course be taken through any of the brilliance zones of the sphere.

In the center of the sphere, the series of grays extends along the axis between the white and black poles. Our diagram, as has been mentioned, has only seven degrees of brilliance. The fourth degree must therefore correspond to the middle gray between white and black, and that middle gray is the center of the sphere.

The same gray is obtained by mixing any two complementaries. Therefore if we take two opposite hues of the equatorial zone, we get a complete set of gradations, as we did in Figs. 23–28 and in the section on complementary colors. In the horizontal cross sections of the color sphere, we confine ourselves to five intermediates between opposite extremes, the central mixture being neutral gray.

Fig. 52 shows a vertical section of the color sphere, taken in the red-orange/blue-green sector. Looking at the equatorial zone of this section, we find blue-green at the left and red-orange at the right in maximum saturation. Towards the axis, we find two mixed degrees of each of the two saturated hues. The resulting seven equatorial chromas are tinted towards white and shaded towards black. Such vertical sections may be passed through any pair of complementary colors and the black and white poles. The several tonalities of any level of lightness or darkness should in this case be equal, and match the gray of that level.

By painting all the horizontal and vertical sections of the sphere in this manner, we complete our color catalogue. Horizontal sections contain the degrees of saturation of the hues, and vertical sections contain the tints and shades of a given pair of complementaries, pure and diluted. Such exercises heighten color sensitivity to light-dark values and to degrees of saturation.

The following, then, are the colors we can construct by means of the color sphere:

1) The pure prismatic hues, located on the equator of the spherical surface;

2) All mixtures of the prismatic hues with white and black, in the brilliance zones of the surface;

3) The mixtures of each complementary pair, as exhibited in a horizontal section;

4) The mixtures of any complementary pair, tinted and shaded towards white and black, as represented in the corresponding vertical section.

Suppose we have a double-pointed needle universally pivoted at the center of the color sphere. Let one point of the needle be directed at any spot on the sphere; then the other point will indicate the symmetrical spot, or complementary color value. If one end points at the second tint of red, namely pink, then the other end will point at the second shade of the complementary green. If we point one end at the second shade of orange, namely brown, then the other will point at the second tint of blue. Thus not only the opposite hues but also all their degrees of brilliance are in complementary relation to each other.

Fig. 53 shows the five principal paths of transition between two contrasting colors. If we begin with a complementary pair, say orange and blue-green, and try to find intermediates between the two, we first locate the two colors on the color sphere. Orange, which lies on the equator, may be modified towards blue

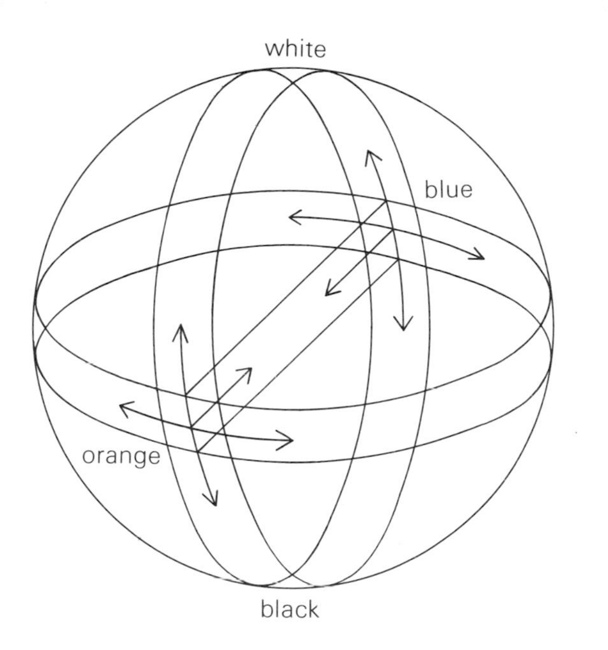

53 Five principal routes between two contrasting colors

along the equator by way of red and violet or else by way of yellow and green. These are the two horizontal paths. Alternatively, the same orange can be connected with blue along the meridian, either by way of light orange, white, and light blue, or else by way of dark orange, black, and dark blue. These are the two vertical paths.

By following the diameter of the color sphere from orange to blue, the two complementaries may be joined by way of gray and other mixtures of orange and blue, in the order of orange-gray, gray, and blue-gray. This is the diagonal path.

These five principal paths are the shortest and simplest lines of transition between the two contrasting hues.

If it be imagined that this systematic classification of colors and contrasts banishes all difficulties, I should add that the kingdom of colors has within it multidimensional possibilities only partly to be reduced to simple order. Each individual color is a universe in itself. We must therefore content ourselves with an exposition of fundamentals.

By color harmony I mean the craft of developing themes from systematic color relationships capable of serving as a basis for composition. Since it would be impossible to catalogue all combinations here, let us confine ourselves to developing some of the harmonic relationships.

Color chords may be formed of two, three, four, or more tones. We shall refer to such chords as dyads, triads, tetrads etc.

1. Dyads

In the 12-hue color circle, two diametrically opposed colors are complementary. They form a harmonious dyad. Red/green, blue/orange, yellow/violet are such dyads. If I use the color sphere, I can get an indefinite number of harmonious dyads. The only requirement is that the two tones be symmetrical with respect to the center of the sphere. Thus if I take a tint of red, the corresponding green must be shaded in the same degree as the red is lightened.

2. Triads

If three hues are selected from the color circle so that their positions form an equilateral triangle, those hues form a harmonious triad.

Yellow/red/blue is the clearest and most powerful of such triads. I should be inclined to call it the fundamental triad. The secondary colors, orange/violet/green, form another distinctive triad.

Yellow-orange/red-violet/blue-green, or red-orange/blue-violet/yellow-green, are other triads whose arrangement in the color circle is an equilateral triangle.

If one color in the complementary dyad yellow/violet is replaced by its two neighbors, thus associating yellow with blue-violet and red-violet, or violet with yellow-green and yellow-orange, the resulting triads are likewise harmonious in character. Their geometrical figure is an isosceles triangle, as Fig. 54 shows. These equilateral and isosceles triangles may also be thought of as inscribed in the color sphere. They may be rotated at will. Provided the point of intersection of the bisectors of their sides lies at the center of the sphere, the three colors related by their vertices make a harmonious triad. Two limiting cases occur when one vertex of the triangle is at white or black. If we use an equilateral triangle with one vertex at white, the other two vertices will point to the first shades of a pair of complementary hues. Then we get such a triad as white/dark blue-green/dark orange. Similarly, for black we get light blue and light orange.

These limiting cases illustrate how light-dark contrast will assume prominence when white or black is used.

3. Tetrads

If we choose two pairs of complementaries in the color circle whose connecting diameters are perpendicular to each other, we obtain a square, as in Fig. 55. The three tetrads of this kind in the 12-hue circle are:

yellow/violet/red-orange/blue-green
yellow-orange/blue-violet/red/green
orange/blue/red-violet/yellow-green

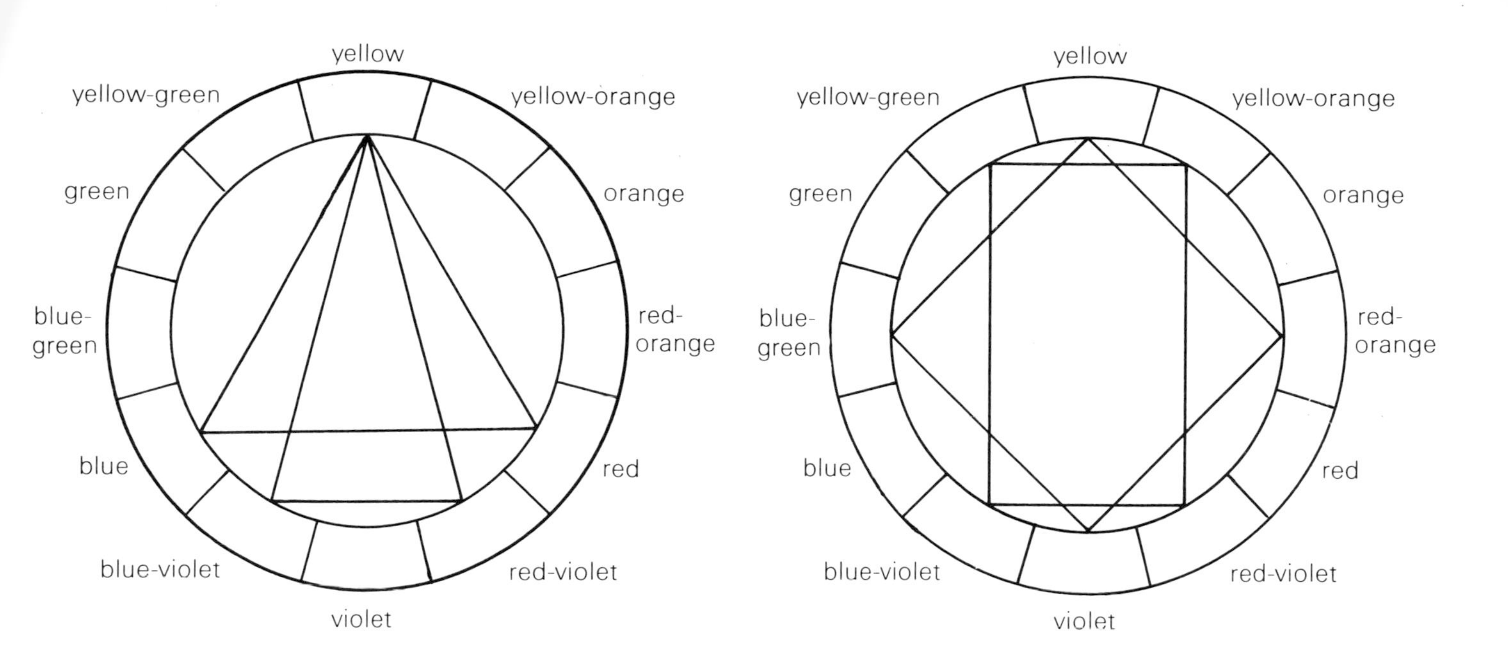

54 Constructions for harmonious triads in the twelve-part color circle

55 Constructions for harmonious tetrads in the twelve-part color circle

More tetrads are obtained with a rectangle containing two complementary pairs:
yellow-green/red-violet/yellow-orange/blue-violet
yellow/violet/orange/blue
A third geometrical figure for harmonious tetrads is the trapezoid. Two hues may be adjacent, and two opposing ones found to the right and left of their complements. The resulting chords tend to simultaneous modification, but they are harmonious; for when mixed, they produce gray-black.
By inscribing the polygons shown in Fig. 55 in a color sphere and rotating them, a very large number of further themes could be derived.

4. Hexads
Hexads may be derived in two different ways.
A hexagon, rather than a square or triangle, may be inscribed in the color circle. Three pairs of complementary colors are then obtained as a harmonious hexad. There are two such hexads in the 12-hue circle:
yellow/violet/orange/blue/red/green
yellow-orange/blue-violet/red-orange/blue-green/red-violet/yellow-green
This hexagon may be rotated in the color sphere. The resulting tints and shades yield interesting color combinations.

The other way to construct a hexad is to adjoin white and black to four pure colors. We place a square in the equatorial plane of the color sphere, obtaining a tetrad of two complementary pairs. Then each vertex of the square is joined to white above and black below, as shown in Fig. 56. The result is a regular octahedron.
Any tetrad obtainable in the equatorial plane may thus be expanded into a hexad by inclusion of white and black.

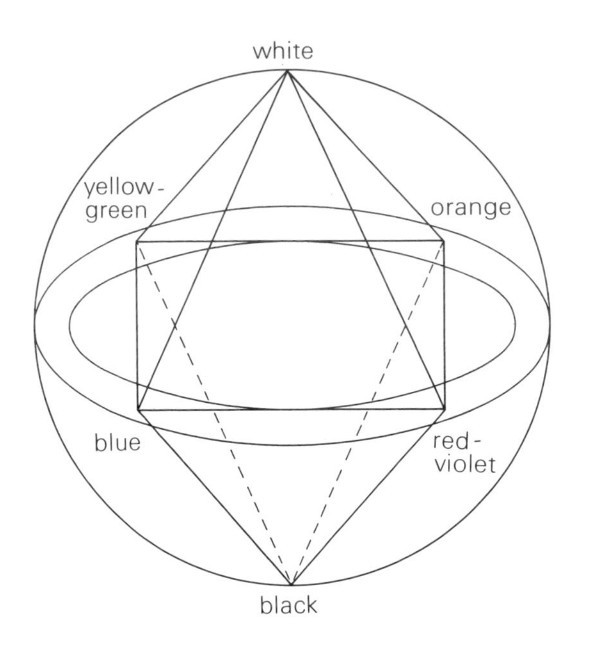

56 The octahedron as a figure for constructing harmonious hexads in the color sphere

A rectangle may be used instead of a square; and an equatorial triangle combined with white and black yields pentads, such as yellow/red/blue/black/white or orange/violet/green/black/white, etc.
Now that these elements of a color harmony have been suggested, it should again be emphasized that the choice of a chord and its modulation as the basis of a composition cannot be arbitrary. All procedures are governed by the subject matter, presented representationally or abstractly. The choice of a theme and its execution are a must, not a capricious will or a superficial maybe. Each color and each group of colors is an individual of unique kind, living and growing according to its immanent law.
The idea of color harmony is to discover the strongest effects by correct choice of antitheses.

In terms of the fundamental chord yellow/red/blue that we discussed in our theory of harmony, let us show how the most diverse variations and effects can be developed from a geometrically constructed theme. One variation consists in placing yellow between blue and red, or red between yellow and blue, or blue between yellow and red. The hues of the fundamental chord can be combined with their shades, producing contrast of saturation. All three colors may be taken in tints and shades, for light-dark contrast. If all three colors are lightened to the same brilliance, and the pure colors added in small areas, a harmony in contrast of extension results. If one color predominates quantitatively, timbres of expressive value are obtained.
By going on to replace a pure color of the chord by its immediate neighbors in the color circle, thus substituting yellow-green and yellow-orange for yellow, or red-orange and red-violet for red, or blue-green and blue-violet for blue, the triad is expanded into a tetrad, greatly enlarging the wealth of variations.
These suggestions are intended to show that a theory of harmony does not tend to fetter the imagination, but on the contrary provides a guide to discovery of new and different means of color expression.

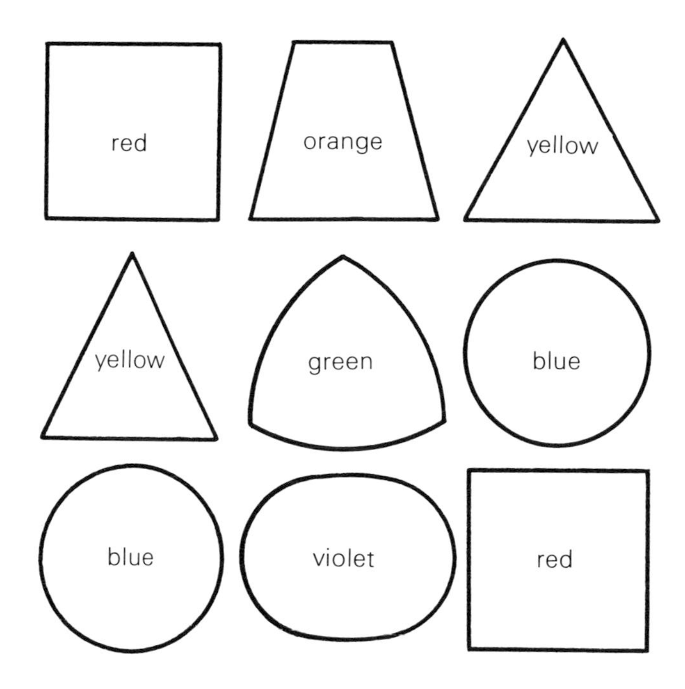

57 Association of colors with corresponding shapes

In the section on theory of color expression, I shall attempt to describe the expressive potentialities of colors. However, shapes also have their "ethico-aesthetic", expressive values.
In a pictorial work, these expressive qualities of form and color should be synchronized; that is, form and color expressions should support each other.

As is true of the three primary colors, red, yellow and blue, the three fundamental shapes – square, triangle, and circle – may be assigned distinct expressive values.

The square, whose essence is two horizontal and two vertical intersecting lines of equal length, symbolizes matter, gravity, and sharp limitation. The Egyptian hieroglyph for "field" is a square. A marked tension is felt when the straight sides and right angles of the square are drawn and experienced as motion. All shapes characterized by horizontals and verticals may be assimilated to square form, including the cross, the rectangle, the Greek key, and their derivatives.
The square corresponds to red, the color of matter. The weight and opacity of red agree with the static and grave shape of the square.

The triangle owes its nature to three intersecting diagonals. Its acute angles produce an effect of pugnacity and aggression. The triangle assimilates all shapes of diagonal character, such as the rhombus, trapezoid, zig-zag, and their derivatives. It is the symbol of thought, and among colors its weightless character is matched by lucid yellow.

A circle is the locus of a point moving at constant distance from a given point in a plane. In contradistinction to the sharp, tense sensation of motion produced by the square, the circle generates a feeling of relaxation and smooth motion. It is the symbol of the spirit, moving

undivided within itself. The ancient Chinese used circular elements to build their temples, while the palace of the temporal sovereign was constructed in quadrangular manner. The astrological symbol for the sun is a circle with a dot in the center.
The circle comprehends all shapes of flexuous, cyclic character, as the ellipse, oval, wave, parabola, and their derivatives. The incessantly moving circle corresponds among colors to transparent blue.

To summarize, the square is resting matter; the radiating triangle is thought, and the circle is spirit in eternal motion. If we look for shapes to match the secondary colors, we find the trapezoid for orange, a spherical triangle for green, and an ellipse for violet; Fig.57.

Coordination of given colors with corresponding shapes involves a parallelism. Where colors and shapes agree in their expression, their effects are additive. A picture whose expression is determined chiefly by color should develop its forms from color, while a picture stressing form should have a coloration derived from its form. The Cubists were most particularly interested in form and reduced their colors in number accordingly. Expressionists and Futurists used both form and color as expressive media; Impressionists dissolved form in favor of color.
What has been said of subjective color holds also of form. Each individual's constitution endows him with certain traits. Graphology inquires into the relationship between subjective form in handwriting and the personality of the writer, but only certain subjective forms can manifest themselves in lineal script.
The Chinese calligraphers admired works of subjective originality, but a scroll was most esteemed if at once original and harmoniously balanced. Brush-and-ink painting was similarly regarded. Liang K'ai and other masters went a step further. They placed no value on originality and personal style; they sought the absolute in art, and attempted to give each subject a formal expression of general validity. Liang K'ai's works differ so in line and tone that it is not easy to identify the artist. Subjectivity of form is submerged in his paintings in the interest of a higher, objective fidelity.
In European painting, Matthias Grünewald aspired to the same objectivity, in form and color. Konrad Witz and El Greco were largely objective as to color, but subjective as to form. De La Tour's work is subjective in form and color alike. Van Gogh's paintings, also, are subjective in both draftsmanship and coloration.
Painting is rich in objective categories. They lie in spatial direction, distribution of mass, free selection of forms and areas with their tonalities and textures.

The spatial effect of a color may be a resultant of several components. Forces acting in the direction of depth are present in the color itself. They may manifest themselves in light-dark, cold-warm, saturation or extension. In addition, a spatial effect may be produced by diagonals and overlappings.

When the six hues, yellow, orange, red, violet, blue, and green, are juxtaposed, without intervals, on a black ground, the light yellow plainly appears to advance, while violet lurks in the depth of the black background. All the other hues are intermediate between yellow and violet. A white background will alter the depth effect. Violet seems to advance from the white ground which holds back the yellow with its kindred brilliance. These observations show how the background color is as essential to depth effect as the applied color. Here we have another instance of the relativity of color effects, discussed in the sections on agents and effects, simultaneous contrast, and color expression.

Back in 1915, studies of depth effect in colors led me to the conclusion that the six fundamental hues on a black ground conform to the ratio of the Golden Section in their gradation of depth.

To divide a line segment according to the Golden Section, let the shorter part bear the same proportion to the longer as the longer bears to the whole length. If the Golden Section of a segment AB is at C, then AC (the shorter part) is to CB as CB is to AB. AC is called the "minor" and CB the "major."

When orange is interposed in the depth interval from yellow to red, the depth intervals from yellow to orange and from orange to red are as minor to major. Similarly, the intervals from yellow to red-orange and from red-orange to blue are as minor to major. Yellow-to-red and red-to-violet are in the same proportion. Yellow-to-green and green-to-blue are as major to minor.

When yellow, red-orange and blue are placed on a black background, the following movements in depth occur: yellow advances sharply, red less so, and blue retreats almost as far as the black. When the same

colors are on white, the depth effect is reversed: blue is driven forward by the white ground, red-orange also, and yellow stands out only slightly from the white. The depth relations of yellow/red-orange and red-orange/blue are as major to minor.
Any light tones on a black ground will advance according to their degree of brilliance. On a white ground, the effect is reversed; light tones are held to the plane of the background, and shades approaching black are thrust forward in corresponding degree.
Among cold and warm tones of equal brilliance, the warm will advance and the cold retreat. If light-dark contrast is also present, the forces in the direction of depth will be added or subtracted or will cancel out. When equally brilliant blue-green and red-orange are seen against black, the blue-green retreats and the red-orange advances. If the red-orange is lightened somewhat, it advances still further. If the blue-green is lightened, it advances to the same level as the red-orange; if lightened sufficiently, it advances further and the red-orange recedes.

The depth effects of saturation contrast are as follows: a pure color advances relative to a duller one of equal brilliance, but if light-dark or cold-warm contrast is also present, the depth relationship shifts accordingly.
Extension is another factor of depth effect. When a large red area bears a small yellow patch, the red acts as a background and the yellow advances. As the yellow is extended and encroaches on the red, a point is reached where the yellow becomes dominant; it expands into a background and thrusts the red forward.
Even if we were to analyze all possible depth effects of color combinations, it would give us no guarantee of spatial equilibrium in a color composition. The individual discrimination and intention of the artist must govern.

To assess colors as factors of depth, one must train one's vision in these comparisons. "Ne faites pas des fenêtres!" said Corot – no holes in the picture; or let us say, painters must be careful of depth effects.

The study of color impression properly begins with color effects in nature. That is, we investigate the impressions made by colored objects on our sense of vision.

One day in 1922, shortly after Kandinsky's appointment to the faculty of the government Bauhaus at Weimar, Gropius, Kandinsky, Klee and I were talking when Kandinsky turned to Klee and myself and asked, "What subjects are you teaching?" Klee said he was lecturing on problems of form, and I explained about my introductory course. Kandinsky rejoined dryly, "Good, then I'll teach nature study!" We nodded, and nothing more was said about the curriculum. For a number of years after this, Kandinsky gave instruction in analytical studies from nature.

It is symptomatic of a lack of orientation in art schools today that the necessity of nature study can be debated.

Nature study in art should not be an imitative reproduction of fortuitous impressions of nature, but rather an analytical, exploratory development and production of the forms and colors needed for true characterization. Such studies do not imitate, but interpret. In order for this interpretation to be pertinent, close observation and clear thinking must precede it. The senses are sharpened, and the artistic intellect is trained in rational analysis of the observed subject matter. The student must take the field against nature, for her powers of presentation are different from and superior to the artist's means of representation. Cézanne worked indefatigably with natural subjects. Van Gogh was destroyed in this struggle, never having compromised his effort to turn his responses to nature into paintings that meaningfully integrated form and color.

Each artist must decide the scope of his nature study, according to his own needs. However, it would be unwise to neglect the external world, from a superabundance of "inner life".

Nature in its rhythm of the seasons, turning now outward, now inward, might well serve as a model for our individual lives. In spring and summer, the forces of earth press outward in growth and maturation; in fall and winter they turn inward and renew themselves.

Let us now consider the problem of colors in nature.

Physically speaking, objects have no color. When white light – by which we mean sunlight – strikes the surface of an object, the latter, according to its molecular constitution, will absorb certain wave lengths, or colors, and reflect others.

In the section on color physics, it was stated that the colors of the spectrum may be divided into two groups in any way, and each group united into one color by means of a converging lens. The resulting two colors are complementary to each other. The rays of light reflected from a surface therefore constitute a color complementary to the color of the absorbed rays. The reflected color appears to us as the intrinsic or local color of the object.

A body that reflects all wave lengths of white light and absorbs none looks white. A body that absorbs all wave lengths of white light and reflects none looks black.

If we illuminate a blue body with orange light, it will look black because orange contains no blue for it to reflect. This demonstrates the primacy of the color of the incident light. Change the color of the lighting, and the local colors of the objects illuminated will change. The more chromatic the lighting, the more the intrinsic colors are modified. The whiter the lighting, the more purely the unabsorbed wave lengths are reflected, and the purer the intrinsic colors appear. Attention to color of illumination is essential in the study of color in nature. We may recall the procedure of the Impressionists who studied the modifications of local colors in continually changing light.

Of course, the intensity of the light is important as well as its color. Light is the cause, not only of the coloration of objects, but also of their plastic corporeality. We shall here distinguish three different intensities, to be called full light, medium light, and shadow.

The local color of objects is most effective in medium light, and details of surface texture are most clearly visible. Full light whitens the intrinsic color, while shadow obscures and darkens it.

Colored light reflected from colored objects variously modifies the colors of other objects.

Every colored object reflects its color into the surrounding space. If such an object is red, and if its red light falls upon a nearby white object, the latter will show reddish reflection. If the red rays strike a green object, the latter will show some gray, since green and red extinguish each other. If the red rays strike a black surface, black-brown reflection will appear.

The glossier the surface, the more conspicuous these reflections will be.

The Impressionist painters, in studying the alterations of intrinsic colors by the changing color of sunlight and of reflections, became convinced that local colors are dissolved in a total atmosphere of color.

So we find that we have four main problems to deal with in the study of color impressions – intrinsic color, color of illumination, shadow, and reflection.

An object may be represented in a variety of ways. It may be drawn in top view, front view, and side view, to an exact scale of dimensions; this is an analytical form of representation. Then again, an object may be delineated in perspective, or modeled in light and shade.

A red vase and a yellow box may be drawn in perspective and their local colors painted flat. The shapes and colors may then be modeled with light and shade. The plastic effect can be flattened again by tying the tonal values of the object to the picture plane with values of like brilliance in the background. In this way the object shades are connected to the surface of the painting.

When each object and each area is assigned its proper local color, a realistic, concrete effect is obtained. Such a composition will consist of a multiplicity of elements that only reluctantly unite into a coherent whole. Konrad Witz often made use of this mode.

When the colors of objects are introduced into the composition as local colors, each object being set in its own colors, red in red, yellow in yellow, the objects are released from their bounded isolation. They dissolve in their own atmosphere, which becomes the picture atmosphere.
Plastic effects may also be obtained by means of cold-warm modulations. Intrinsic colors begin to be dissolved. Variations of light and shade are replaced by equivalent colder or warmer variations of the local colors. Light-dark contrast is largely eliminated, and an effect of pictorial atmosphere results.

Local colors may be studied as modified by the color of the incident light. In bluish light, a green vase will look blue-green and a yellow dish yellow-green, because the intrinsic colors mix with the hue of the light.

Reflections break up local tones and dissolve the shapes and colors of objects in a polyphony of patches.
Delacroix said that all nature is reflection.

Colored shadows are another topic in the study of color impressions.

When shadows of trees are observed on a summer evening in the orange light of sunset, while the eastern sky is clear, the blue color may be seen very plainly. Colored shadows can be observed still more easily in winter, when snow lies in the streets. Under a dark-blue night sky, in the orange light of street lamps, deep blue, luminous shadows are seen on the snow. Passing along a busy shopping street with many-colored displays after a snow, one may see red, green, blue and yellow shadows on the ground.

In painting, an attack on this problem was made by the Impressionists. Blue shadows of trees in their paintings caused great excitement among visitors at exhibitions. The common opinion had been that shadows should be painted gray-black. But the Impressionists had arrived at the representation of colored shadows by minute observation of nature.

However, the term "impression" as used here is not restricted to the Impressionist school of painting. The Van Eycks, Holbein, Velásquez, Zurbarán, the Le Nain brothers, Chardin, and Ingres all painted impressionally in that their works are informed by close observation of nature.
Chinese brush-and-ink painting is also in large part impressional. Characteristic philosophical attitudes involved veneration of nature and natural forces. Not surprisingly, therefore, painters devoted thorough study to the forms of nature. Mountains, water, trees, flowers, became aesthetic symbols. The Chinese painter studies natural forms until he masters them like written characters. To represent these natural forms, he commonly employs but one pigment, black ink, which he modulates in all possible shades. The abstract connotation of black ink intensifies the fundamentally symbolic character of his painting.

In contemporary painting, human faces may show green, blue, or violet. People are often at a loss to account for these unnatural colors. There are various reasons that may prompt a painter to use colors in this manner.

Blue and violet in a face may have expressive significance, representing a psychological state. Again, a green or blue face may have symbolic meaning. Such devices are not new. Symbolic complexion is found at an early period in both Indian and Mexican painting. Or, green or blue in a face may represent the shadow effect of a corresponding color of illumination.

The following experiments may help to clarify the problem of colored shadows. In 1944, I had occasion to demonstrate this phenomenon in connection with an exhibition at the Zurich Museum of Arts and Crafts. A white object was illuminated, in daylight, with red light; a green shadow resulted. Green light produced a red shadow, yellow light a violet shadow, and violet light a yellow shadow.

In daylight, each colored light produced a shadow of the complementary color. I asked Hans Finsler, the photographer, to take pictures of this phenomenon. Color photos showed that the colored shadows were really present, and not due simply to simultaneous contrast. All the mixtures of colors in such experiments correspond to additive color syntheses, being mixtures of light rather than of pigments.

In further experiments with colored shadows, the following surprising results were obtained:

1) In red light, in the absence of daylight, a black shadow was produced. Shadows in blue and green illumination were likewise black.

2) The object was illuminated with two colored lights in the absence of daylight. In the case of red and green lights, the red light produced green shadows, and vice versa. The intersection of the two shadows was black, and the mixture of green and red light was yellow. When red-orange and blue-green light was used, the red-orange light produced a blue-green shadow, and vice versa. The intersection of the shadows was black, and the mixture of the two illuminating colors was lavender. When the illuminating colors were green and blue, the green light produced a blue shadow, and vice versa. The intersection of the shadows was black, and the mixed light was blue-green.

3) When three illuminating colors, red-orange, green and blue-green, were used, the red-orange light produced a blue-green shadow, the green light produced a lavender shadow, and the blue-green light produced a yellow shadow. The intersection of the three shadows was black. The mixture of the three colored lights produced a white background.

Impressional studies offer the artist many opportunities to interpret the marvels of form and color found in nature.

The optical, electromagnetic, and chemical processes initiated in the eye and brain are frequently paralleled by processes in the psychological realm. Such reverberations of the experience of color may be propagated to the inmost centers, thereby affecting principal areas of mental and emotional experience. Goethe spoke of the ethico-aesthetic activity of colors. By careful analysis, I shall try to elucidate this topic, so important to the color artist.

I recall the following anecdote:
A businessman was entertaining a party of ladies and gentlemen at dinner. The arriving guests were greeted by delicious smells issuing from the kitchen, and all were eagerly anticipating the meal. As the happy company assembled about the table, laden with good things, the host flooded the apartment with red light. The meat looked rare and appetizing enough, but the spinach turned black and the potatoes were bright red. Before the guests had recovered from their astonishment, the red light changed to blue, the roast assumed an aspect of putrefaction, and the potatoes looked moldy. All the diners lost their appetite at once; but when the yellow light was turned on, transforming the claret into castor oil and the company into living cadavers, some of the more delicate ladies hastily rose and left the room. No one could think of eating, though all present knew it was only a change in the color of the lighting. The host laughingly turned the white lights on again, and soon the good spirits of the gathering were restored. Who can doubt that colors exert profound influences upon us, whether we are aware of them or not?
The deep blue of the sea and distant mountains enchants us; the same blue as an interior seems uncanny, lifeless, and terrifying. Blue reflections on the skin render it pale, as if moribund. In the dark of night, a blue neon light is attractive, like blue on black, and in conjunction with red and yellow lights it lends a cheerful, lively tone. A blue sunfilled sky has an active and en-

livening effect, whereas the mood of the blue moonlit sky is passive and evokes subtle nostalgias.

Redness in the face denotes wrath or fever; a blue, green, or yellow complexion, sickness, though there is nothing sickly about the pure colors. A red sky threatens bad weather; a blue, green, or yellow sky promises fair weather.

On the basis of these experiences of nature, it would seem all but impossible to formulate simple and true propositions about the expressive content of colors.

Yellow shadows, violet light, blue-green fire, red-orange ice, are effects in apparent contradiction with experience, and give an other-worldly expression. Only those deeply responsive can experience the tonal values of single or simultaneous colors without reference to objects. Musical experience is denied to those with no ear for music.

The example of the four seasons shows that color sensation and experience have objective correlatives, even though each individual sees, feels, and evaluates color in a very personal way. I have often maintained that the judgment "pleasing-displeasing" can be no valid criterion of true and correct coloration. A serviceable yardstick is obtained only if we base each judgment on the relation and relative position of each color with respect to the adjacent color and the totality of colors. Stated in terms of the four seasons, this means that for each season we are to find those colors, those points on and in the color sphere, that distinctly belong to the expression of that season in their relation to the whole universe of colors.

The youthful, light, radiant generation of nature in spring is expressed by luminous colors. Yellow is the color nearest to white light, and yellow-green is its intensification. Light pink and light blue tones amplify and enrich the chord. Yellow, pink, and lilac are often seen in the buds of plants.

The colors of autumn contrast most sharply with those of spring. In autumn, the green of vegetation dies out, to be broken down and decomposed into dull brown and violet.

The promise of spring is fulfilled in the maturity of summer.

Nature in summer, thrust materially outward into a maximum luxuriance of form and color, attains extreme density and a vividly plastic fullness of powers. Warm, saturated, active colors, to be found at their peak in only one particular region of the color sphere, offer themselves for the expression of summer. For contrast with and amplification of these principal colors, their complements will of course also be required.

To represent winter, typifying passivity in nature by a contracting, inward movement of the forces of earth, we require colors connoting withdrawal, cold and centripetal radiance, transparency, rarefaction.

The majestic cycle of respiration performed by nature in these four phases can hence be clearly and objectively represented in color; but unless we apply reason to the choice of color combinations, keeping the total universe of color before us, we shall find none but private solutions, and miss those of general truth and validity.

In order to gain an understanding of each hue in its unique psychological, expressive value, let us relate it to the other hues. To avoid error insofar as possible, we must know, when mentioning any color, precisely what chroma and what tone are meant, and with what color it is to be related. When I say "red", I must specify which red, as well as the color to be related to it. A yellowish red, such as red-orange, is different in species from a bluish red, and red-orange on lemon-yellow is again a very different matter from red-orange on black, or on its equal in brilliance, lilac.

I shall now try to relate the hues yellow, red, blue, orange, violet and green as represented and defined in the 12-hue color circle of Fig. 3, and to describe their mental and emotional expressive values.

Yellow

Yellow is the most light-giving of all hues. It loses this

trait the moment we shade it with gray, black, or violet. Yellow is, as it were, a denser, material white. The further this yellowed light is drawn into the denseness of matter, of opacity, the more it is assimilated to yellow-orange, orange and red-orange. Our red is the stopping point of yellow, with which it is not visibly tinged. In the center of the yellow-to-red band, we have orange, as the strongest and most concentrated interpenetration of light and matter. Golden yellow suggests the highest sublimation of matter by the power of light, impalpably radiant, lacking transparency, but weightless as a pure vibration. Gold was formerly much used in painting. It signifies luminous, light-emitting matter. The golden domes of Byzantine mosaics and the backgrounds in the paintings of early masters were symbols of the beyond, the marvelous, the kingdom of sun and light. The golden aura of saints is the token of their transfiguration. The attainment of this state was conceived as an envelopment by light. This heavenly light could not be symbolized except by gold.
In common speech, to "see the light" means to be brought to a realization of previously hidden truth. To say that someone is "bright" is to credit him with intelligence. So yellow, the brightest and lightest color, pertains symbolically to understanding, knowledge. In Grünewald's conception, the risen Christ ascends in a glory of yellow. Yellow is used in the sense of celestial light in Altdorfer's "Madonna and Child with Angels."

Just as there is but one truth, so there is only one yellow. Adulterated truth is vitiated truth, untruth. So the expressions of diluted yellow are envy, betrayal, falseness, doubt, distrust, and unreason. In Giotto's "Taking of Christ" and in Holbein's "Last Supper", Judas is shown in dim yellow. The gray-yellow cloak of a female figure in the "Stripping of Christ" by El Greco has a peculiarly mistrustful effect.
On the other hand, yellow is radiantly cheerful when contrasted with dark tones.

Figs. 60–63 show how the same yellow may be altered in expression by different juxtaposed colors.
With yellow on pink, the radiance of the yellow is subdued.

With yellow on orange, the yellow looks like a purer, lighter orange. The two colors together are like strong morning sun on ripening wheatfields.
Yellow on green gives a radiant effect, outshining the green. Since green is a mixture of yellow and blue, the yellow is among friends.
Yellow on violet has an extreme strength of character, hard and inexorable.
Yellow on medium blue is radiant but alien and repellent in effect. Sentimental blue will not readily tolerate the bright wit of yellow.
Yellow on red is a loud joyful noise, like trumpets on Easter Morn. Its splendor sends forth a mighty knowledge and affirmation.
Yellow on white is dim and without radiance. The white forces it into a subservient position.
Yellow shows its brightest and most aggressive luminosity on black. It is vigorous and sharp, uncompromising and abstract.
The various effects of yellow well illustrate the difficulty of defining the expressive properties of colors in general terms without direct intuition.

Red

The red of the 12-hue color circle is neither yellowish nor bluish. Its irresistible radiancy is not easily eclipsed, and yet is extraordinarily flexible, bordering on diverse characters. It is very sensitive where it shifts into yellowish or into bluish. Both yellowish red and bluish red unfold great capacity for modulation.
Red-orange is dense and opaque, glowing as if filled with inner warmth. The warmness of red is intensified to fiery strength in red-orange. It is symbolically comparable to vitalized earth. Red-orange light promotes vegetable growth and organic function.
Proper contrasting turns red-orange into an expression

of feverish, belligerent passion. Associated with the planet Mars, red is bound to the burning worlds of war and demons. It was worn as a sign of material occupation by warriors in combat. It has been the badge of revolutions.

Passionate physical love glows forth in red-orange; blue-red purple connotes spiritual love. Thus Charonton portrayed the Father and the Son in crimson robes. The Madonna of the Isenheim altarpiece and the Madonna of Stuppach, by Grünewald, are both clad in red.

In purple, the color of the cardinals, temporal and spiritual power are united.

By varying color contrasts with red-orange, I try to show in Figs. 64–67 how a red may be expressively modified.

On orange, red-orange seems smoldering, dark and lifeless, as if parched. If the orange is deepened to dark brown, the fire of the red flares with a dry heat. It is only in contrast with black that fire red develops its utmost unconquerable, demonic passion. On green, red-orange is an impudent, rash intruder, loud and common. On green-blue, red-orange is like a blazing fire. On a cold red, it drops back to a subdued glow, driving the red to active resistance.

The different effects of red-orange in our examples are only a suggestion of its expressive potentialities. Unlike yellow, red has a great wealth of modulations because it can be widely varied between cold and warm, dull and clear, light and dark, without destroying its character of redness. From demonic, sinister red-orange on black, to sweet angelic pink, red can express all intermediate degrees between the infernal and the sublime. Only the ethereal, transparent, aerial is barred to it, for there blue reigns supreme.

Blue

Pure blue is a color containing no trace of yellow or red.

As red is always active, so blue is always passive, from

Color Agent and Color Effect

58 Yellow squares of equal size look bigger on white than on black

59 Red squares of equal size look smaller than on black

60–71 Combinations showing how the same yellow, red and blue are altered in expression by different juxtaposed colors

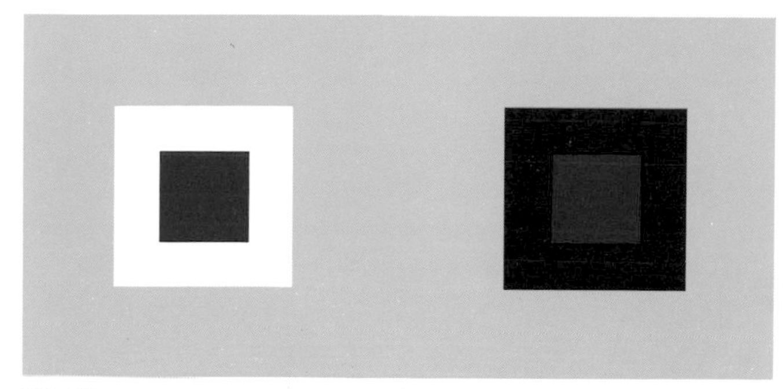

58–59

60–63

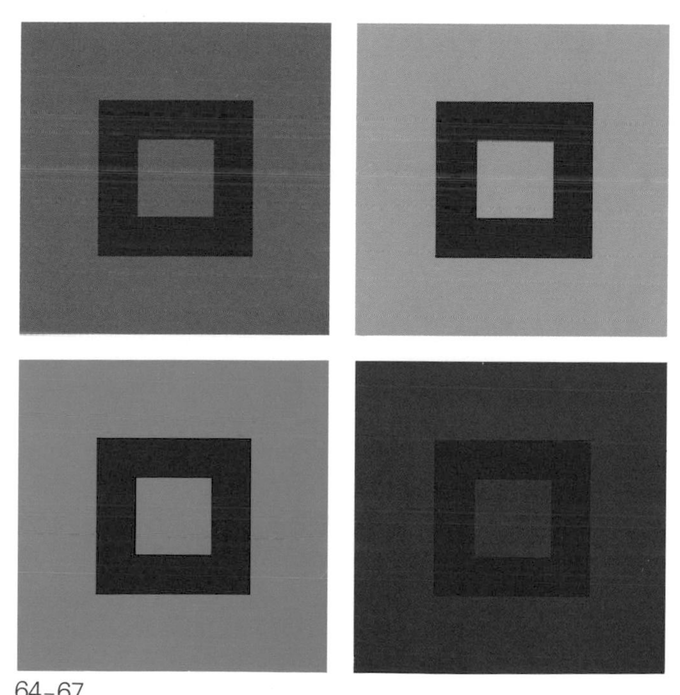

64–67

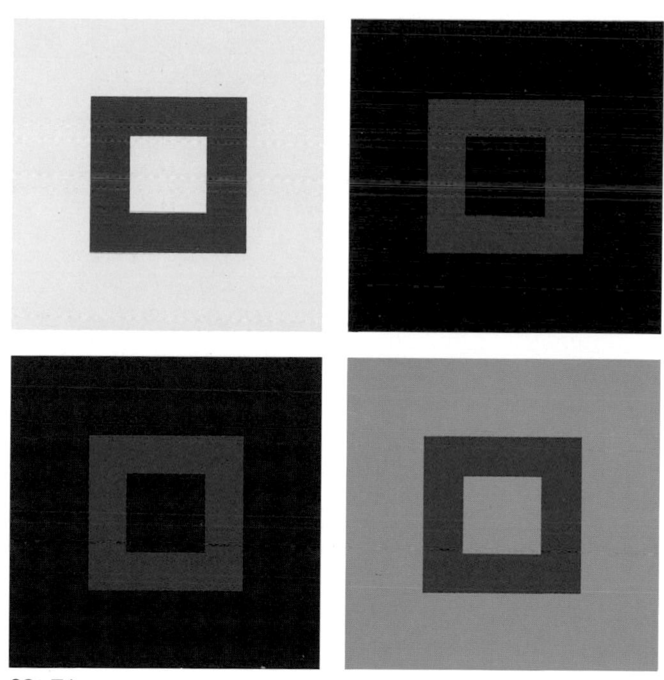

68–71

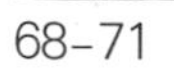

the point of view of material space. From the point of view of spiritual immateriality, blue seems active and red passive. Blue is always cold, and red is always warm. Blue is contracted, introverted. As red is associated with blood, so is blue with the nervous system.
Blue is a power like that of nature in winter, when all germination and growth is hidden in darkness and silence. Blue is always shadowy, and tends in its greatest glory to darkness. It is an intangible nothing, and yet present as the transparent atmosphere. In the atmosphere of the earth, blue appears from lightest azure to the deepest blue-black of the night sky. Blue beckons our spirit with the vibrations of faith into the infinite distances of spirit. Signifying faith to us, for the Chinese it symbolized immortality.
When blue is dimmed, it falls into superstition, fear, grief, and perdition, but always it points to the realm of the transcendental.

Figs. 68–71 show changes in the effect of blue with changing color contrast.
Blue on yellow has a very dark effect indeed, devoid of radiance. Where bright intellect rules, faith appears dull and obscure. When the blue is lightened to the same brilliance as the yellow, it casts a cold light. Its transparency demotes yellow to a dense, material hue.
On black, blue gleams in bright, pure strength. Where black ignorance holds sway, the blue of pure faith shines like a distant light.
If we set blue on lilac it appears withdrawn, inane, and impotent. The lilac takes from it all significance by right of the greater material strength of "practical faith." When the lilac is darkened, the blue takes back its luster.
On dark brown (dark, dull orange), blue is excited into a strong vibrant tremor, and the brown simultaneously awakens into live color. The brown that was dead is resurrected by the power of blue.
Blue on red-orange retains its dark figure, yet becomes luminous, asserting and maintaining its strange unreality.
On quiet green, our blue is markedly shifted towards red. Only by this "evasion" can it escape from the paralyzing saturation of the green and return to active life.
The retiring nature of blue, its meekness and profound faith, are frequently encountered in paintings of the Annunciation. The Virgin, hearkening inward, wears blue. A fine example is in Roger van der Weyden's Altar of the Epiphany.

Green

Green is the intermediate between yellow and blue. According as green contains more yellow or more blue, the character of its expression changes. Green is one of the secondary colors, produced by mixing two primaries – an operation difficult to perform in such a way that neither component predominates.
Green is the color of the vegetable kingdom, the mysterious chlorophyll involved in photosynthesis. When light comes to the earth, and water and air release their elements, then incarnate sentience puts forth green. Fruitfulness and contentment, tranquility and hope are expressive values of green, the fusion and interpenetration of knowledge and faith. When luminous green is dulled by gray, a sense of sad decay easily results. If the green inclines towards yellow, coming within the range of yellow-green, we feel the young, vernal force of nature. A spring or early summer morning without yellow-green, without hope and joy for the fruits of summer, is unthinkable.
Yellow-green may be activated to the utmost by orange, though it then readily assumes a coarse, vulgar cast.
If the green inclines towards blue, its spiritual components are augmented. Manganese blue represents the richest hue of blue-green. This ice blue is the cold pole, as red-orange is the warm pole, of our color world. In antithesis to green and blue, it has a cold, vigorous aggressiveness.

The range of modulation of green is very broad, and

many different expressive values can be obtained by variations in contrast.

Orange

Orange, the mixture of yellow and red, is at the focus of maximum radiant activity. It has solar luminosity in the material sphere, attaining the maximum of warm, active energy in reddish orange. Festive orange readily becomes proud external ostentation. Whitened, it quickly loses character; diluted with black, it declines into dull, taciturn, and withered brown. By lightening brown, we obtain beige tones, engendering a warm, beneficent atmosphere in quiet, intimate interiors.

Violet

The difficulty of fixing a precise violet, neither reddish nor bluish, is extreme. Many individuals have no discrimination for shades of violet. As the antipode of yellow, or consciousness, violet is the color of the unconscious – mysterious, impressive, and sometimes oppressive, now menacing, now encouraging, according to contrast. When violet is present in large areas it can be distinctly terrifying, particularly towards the purple. "A light of this kind, cast upon a landscape," says Goethe, "suggests the terrors of the end of the world."

Violet is the hue of piety, and, when darkened and dulled, of dark superstition. Lurking catastrophe bursts forth from dark violet. Once it is lightened, when light and understanding illuminate dark piety, delicate and lovely tints enchant us.

Chaos, death, and exaltation in violet, solitude and dedication in blue-violet, divine love and spiritual dominion in red-violet – these, in few words, are some of the expressive values of the violet band. Many plants have light violet shoots with yellow centers.

Generally speaking, all tints represent the brighter aspects of life, whereas shades symbolize the dark and negative forces.

We can use two tests to check the accuracy of these remarks on the expressive values of colors. If two colors are complementary, their interpretations should be complementary; and when a color is mixed, its interpretation should correspond to the mixture of the interpretations of the original colors.

1. Complementary Pairs
   yellow : violet = bright knowledge : dark, emotional piety
   blue : orange = submissive faith : proud self-respect
   red : green = material force : sympathy

2. Mixed Colors
   red + yellow = orange
   power + knowledge = proud self-respect
   red + blue = violet
   love + faith = piety
   yellow + blue = green
   knowledge + faith = compassion

The more I consider the mentally and emotionally expressive values of colors, the more I realize that the effects of colors and our subjective individuality in receptiveness to color experience are both extremely variable.

Any color may be varied in five modes:

1) In hue; that is, green may become more yellowish or more bluish, orange more yellowish or reddish, etc.

2) In brilliance; that is, red may appear as pink, red, dark red, and blue as light blue, blue, dark blue, etc.

3) In saturation; that is, blue may be more or less diluted with white, black, gray, or its complementary (orange).

4) In extension; a large area of green may lie beside a small area of yellow, or vice versa, or the quantities of yellow and green may be equal.

5) In effects due to simultaneous contrast.

The contents of this section have brought us to a critical point in the process of artistic creation. Perception and experience may be keen, but unless the proper basic group is selected from the totality of colors at the outset, the final effect of the work is jeopardized. Therefore, subconscious perception, intuitive thought, and positive knowledge should always function together, enabling us to choose appropriately from the multiplicity of means available.

Matisse wrote, "Given a correct fundamental attitude, it would turn out that the procedure of making a picture is no less logical than that of building a house. The human aspect need not be considered. One has it or not; if one has it, it will show up in the work anyway."
Examples of expressive coloration are especially abundant in the work of Konrad Witz (1410–1445). I would mention the paintings "Caesar and Antipater", "David and Abishai" and "The Synagogue", all in the Kunstmuseum at Basle. Then there is Pieter Brueghel the Elder's (1525–1569) "Parable of the Blind Men", Naples, Museo Nazionale; and the "Resurrection and Transfiguration of Jesus" from the Isenheim altarpiece by Matthias Grünewald (1470–1528), Colmar, Museum Unterlinden.

To compose in color means to juxtapose two or more colors in such a way that they jointly produce a distinct and distinctive expression. The selection of hues, their relative situation, their locations and orientations within the composition, their configurations or simultaneous patterns, their extensions and their contrast relationships, are decisive factors of expression.
The subject of color composition is so many-faceted that we shall only be able to suggest some of the basic ideas.
Some of the resources for harmonious composition were discussed in the section on harmony. In interpreting the expressive properties of colors (section on color expression), we have tried to state concrete conditions and requirements for the genesis of one characteristic expression or another. The purpose to be served by means of colors must govern their selection.

It is an essential point that the effect of a color is determined by its situation relative to accompanying colors. A color is always to be seen in relation to its surroundings.

The farther a hue is removed from a given hue in the color circle, the greater its power of contrast.
However, the value and importance of a color in the picture are not determined by the accompanying colors alone. Quality and quantity of extension are contributing factors.
Thus the placement and direction of colors is important in pictorial composition. Blue behaves differently at the top, bottom, left, or right of the field. Low blue is heavy, high blue is light. Dark red at the top acts as a heavy, impending weight; at the bottom, as a stable matter of fact. Yellow gives an effect of weightlessness at the top, and of captive buoyancy at the bottom.
To bring about a balance of color distribution is one of the most important aims of composition. As the fulcrum

is necessary to the beam of a pair of scales in order to sustain equilibrium, so the vertical axis of equilibrium is essential in a painting. The weights of color areas act on either side of that axis.
Each of the several possible directions in the field of a painting – horizontal, vertical, diagonal, circular, or combinations of these – has its peculiar expression. "Horizontal" denotes weight, distance, breadth. "Vertical," the strongest antithesis to horizontal, denotes lightness, height, and depth. The two directions together give an effect of area, a feeling of equilibrium, solidity, and material hardness. A strong accent occurs where horizontal and vertical intersect.
"Diagonal" directions generate movement and lead into the depth of the picture. In Grünewald's "Resurrection", the diagonal motion of the shroud throws the gaze from the horizontal foreground up to the perfection of the aura.

Painters of the Baroque period used diagonals in their murals to produce perspective illusions. El Greco, Liss, and Maulpertsch, who developed the expressive moment of their paintings out of directional contrasts of forms and colors, preferred diagonal orientation.
Chinese painters have made conscious use of diagonal movement along with vertical axes to lead the eye into the depths of a landscape, the diagonals often vanishing in misty distance.
The Cubists used diagonal orientation and triangular forms quite differently, to intensify an effect of plastic relief.
"Circular" forms have a concentrating effect, while at the same time producing a feeling of movement.
An excellent example of circular movement is the treatment of the cloud formations in Altdorfer's "Victory of Alexander". They repeat and intensify the excitement of the battle scene.

Many of Titian's paintings modulate the brilliance of colors in horizontal and vertical directions. This distribution of light and dark has therefore been referred to as "Titian's formula". Figures are introduced in diagonal or circular movement.

Human vision is such that we tend to join like to like, and see them jointly. The likeness may be of colors, areas, shades, textures, or accents. During observation, a visual "configuration" is formed. I call this configuration a simultaneous pattern when it results from the presented relations of likeness, without being itself materially present.
Simultaneous patterns may result from two sizes of areas and unlike colors.
The eye tends to put like colors together, so that when the colors are many, several simultaneous patterns may coexist.
The effect of composition depends on the forms, features, directions, and spacing of simultaneous patterns. All simultaneous patterns present should occupy a distinctive situation relative to each other.
The fact that likenesses generate simultaneous patterns is a principle of order and articulation. Just as human society is articulated into relationships of blood, opinion, or status, so relationships are the source of order and clear intelligibility in a picture.

Another way to achieve order in a picture is to organize light and dark or cold and warm color groups into well-defined areas and masses. Clear and distinct arrangement and distribution of the principal contrasts is essential to good composition.
A most important element of order is codirectionality or parallelism. This can be used to interconnect complexes of very different kinds.
When colors are used as masses or areas, they can be intensified by the device known as "displacement". If red and green are represented in two masses, the red may be shifted towards green and the green towards red. Care must be taken that displacements do not disintegrate unified masses or areas and destroy the basic conception.

An important consideration is whether a color shape shall be statically fixed in effect, or dynamic, free floating. This sort of fixation has been called ''permeation'', by a color or shape. In murals, permeation is very useful for stabilizing the composition. It is especially apparent as a principle of composition in Giotto's frescoes.

Much the same stabilization can be achieved by emphasizing a vertical or horizontal within the interior of an unattached form. The vertical or horizontal connects with the boundaries of the picture by parallelism, giving a feeling of static solidity. Pictures constructed in this way seem like self-contained universes. But when such isolation from the surroundings is not wanted, and the painting is to be connected to the world outside and to the infinity of forms and colors, then the boundary must not be accentuated, and the composition should be in a high degree non-directional and frameless.

Many different resources of color composition have been suggested. In the execution of a pictorial idea, however, the flow of intuition should not be dammed up by rigid prescription.

In this book I have tried to build a serviceable conveyance in which the color artist may travel a longish distance upon his way. Yet this will be no easy pilgrimage. The route is fixed by the inexorable laws of color.

These laws shine forth in the rainbow, and are discernible in the artificially constructed color sphere, extending and enlarging the pure hues and their mixtures into the polar regions of black and white.

Black, with its profound obscurity, is necessary in order to set the beams of colored light in a dimension suitable to them. The bright radiance of white is necessary, lending the colors its material strength.

Between black and white, there throbs the universe of chromatic phenomena. So long as colors are bound to the world of objects, we can perceive them and recognize their relationships; their inner esssence remains concealed from our understanding, and must be grasped intuitively. Hence rules and formulae can be no more than signposts on the way to color fulfillment in art.

In his Trattato della Pittura, which sets up a formidable array of rules for painters, Leonardo remarks, "Didst thou attempt to create by rule, thou shouldst accomplish nought, but devise only confusion." Thus he relieved his readers once more of the encumbrance of knowledge, and encouraged them to follow their intuition.

It is not the means of expression and representation that count in art, but the individual in his identity and humanity. First comes the cultivation and creation of the individual; then the individual can create.

The serious study of colors is an excellent means to the cultivation of human beings, for it leads to a perception of inner necessities. To grasp these is to experience the eternal law of all natural generation; to recognize necessity is to surrender self-will and serve the Creator – to become Man.

In this book, I have discussed a number of masterpieces of painting and tried to discover their hidden meanings. I chose old masters chiefly, because many readers may be familiar with the originals. But the color principles they illustrate are timeless, and as valid today as they ever were.

Whoever sees only the subjective and the symbolic content in the paintings of Francesca, Rembrandt, Brueghel, Cézanne, and other masters old and new, to him the gates are closed upon their artistic power and beauty. The end and aim of all artistic endeavor is liberation of the spiritual essence of form and color and its release from imprisonment in the world of objects. It is from this aspiration that non-objective art has arisen. The world we live in today is unlike that known to man in 1560, or 1860. Our world is fashioned by contrivance. We build machines whose meaning lies in their function. Machines are not symbols of ideas, but embodiments of purposeful thought.
Even pictures, today, are not symbolic. They have their raison d'être in themselves, in their forms and colors. The painter uses areas and colors for his own projection; the necessary life force flows from himself. He fashions his experience under the guidance of intuition, or inspiration.
However painting may evolve, color will remain its prime material.

Zurich, February 18, 1961.

Johannes Itten.